To the children: Tayesa, Italo, and Aida; to the woman who knows me best and accepts my passion for life and sports, Benita; and to my Dad, so he will stay inspired and continue his writing.

John Yacenda

To my father, who created and inspired the writer in me; to Rebecca and Devin, who give me their youthful enthusiasm and love of skiing; and to Karin, my constant companion in the mountains whether on skis, mountain bikes, or crampons.

Tim Ross

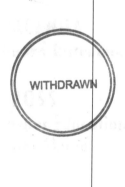

Library of Congress Cataloging-in-Publication Data

Yacenda, John, 1947-
    High-performance skiing / John Yacenda, Tim Ross. -- 2nd ed.
      p.   cm.
    Includes index.
    ISBN 0-88011-713-3
    1. Skis and skiing.   I. Ross, Tim, 1948- . II. Title.
  GV854.Y33   1997
  796.93--dc21
                                                      97-29598
ISBN: 0-88011-713-3   CIP

Acquisitions Editor: Martin Barnard; **Developmental Editor:** Marni Basic; **Assistant Editor:** Henry Woolsey; **Editorial Assistants:** Amy Carnes, Laura Majersky, and Marilyn Sahiba; **Copyeditor:** Cynthia Hastings; **Proofreader:** Tony Callihan; **Indexer:** Mary Prottsman; **Graphic Designer:** Robert Reuther; **Graphic Artist:** Angela K. Snyder; **Photo Editor:** Boyd LaFoon; **Cover Designer:** Jack Davis; **Photographer (cover):** © F-Stock/Mark Gallup; **Mac Art:** Tom Roberts; **Printer:** Versa Press

Photos on pages 48-60 by Tom Roberts. All others by Jane Dove Juneau, except where noted.

Figures 6.2, 6.3, 6.4, 6.5, and 6.6 reprinted, by permission, from ACEP, 1994, *Rookie Coaches Ski Racing Guide* (Champaign, IL: Human Kinetics Publishers), pp. 36-39.

Human Kinetics books are available at special discounts for bulk purchase. Special editions or book excerpts can also be created to specification. For details, contact the Special Sales Manager at Human Kinetics.

Printed in the United States of America   10 9 8 7 6 5 4 3 2 1

Human Kinetics
Web site: http://www.humankinetics.com/

United States: Human Kinetics, P.O. Box 5076, Champaign, IL 61825-5076
1-800-747-4457
e-mail: humank@hkusa.com

Canada: Human Kinetics, Box 24040, Windsor, ON N8Y 4Y9
1-800-465-7301 (in Canada only)
e-mail: humank@hkcanada.com

Europe: Human Kinetics, P.O. Box IW14, Leeds LS16 6TR, United Kingdom
(44) 1132 781708
e-mail: humank@hkeurope.com

Australia: Human Kinetics, 57A Price Avenue, Lower Mitcham, South Australia 5062
(088) 277 1555
e-mail: humank@hkaustralia.com

New Zealand: Human Kinetics, P.O. Box 105-231, Auckland 1
(09) 523 3462
e-mail: humank@hknewz.com

CONTENTS

FOREWORD

There's nothing like flying down a mountain so fast that the run literally opens up before your eyes. I love to rock 'n' roll right out of the starting gate! The success I've had on the World Cup circuit is from having the confidence to ski on the edge—without this faith I lose any chance of winning.

Unfortunately, there are no shortcuts to performance skiing. Standing on the podium as World Downhill Champion was the highlight of a long journey that began when I was a small child in Sun Valley, Idaho. I started working on my racing skills with the Sun Valley Ski Team, and I've been trying to perfect them ever since.

During these many years I have spent thousands of hours on drills, technical progressions, tactical training, physical conditioning, and on developing mental skills—these have been the building blocks that allowed me to excel at ski racing. Mastering the fundamentals gave me the confidence to "go for broke," and all my hard work has paid off on the result sheets.

High-Performance Skiing will give you the building blocks to do your best skiing and handle anything the mountain throws at you. John Yacenda and Tim Ross relate the skills, equipment, conditioning, and strategies that will help you tackle the steeps, bumps, and powder—in all conditions. With these skills, Tim has seen me progress from a fourteen-year-old at the international children's championships through my first top-ten finish and on to World Cup Champion.

To uncover your true potential you must first find your own limits and then have the courage to blow past them! Follow the advice in this book, and you'll be ripping down the mountain in no time.

Picabo Street
Two-Time World Cup Downhill Champion (1995, 1996)
World Downhill Champion (1996)
Four-Time U.S. National Champion

PREFACE

Ten years ago I had a vision for a book about alpine skiing that would be designed and written to offer readers practical advice on how to rev up their skiing in every sort of skiing condition. The product of that endeavor was the first edition of *High-Performance Skiing*. Many elements contributed to the decision to publish a second edition: new breakthroughs in ski technique and physical training, technological advances in alpine equipment, my deeper appreciation for the sport, and Tim's interest in joining me to write this new edition. Together, we've put together a book you'll enjoy— one that promises to further explore high-performance techniques and skills that lead to more consistent performance, less fatigue and more endurance, greater strength and flexibility, greater versatility, increased confidence in the full range of skiing conditions, and the incentive and know-how to jump into serious recreational racing.

This second edition is a brand-new look at the concepts and skills developed in the first edition, with exciting new information on racing, skill development, equipment, and training. The language of the book remains friendly, and we get you on the road toward high-performance skiing right away. As before, some parts of this book deal with perspectives, opinions, strategies, and ideas; the majority of the book, however, focuses on on-the-snow tips and training. *High-Performance Skiing* is an up-front, how-to approach to the best skiing has to offer skiers interested in revving up their skiing and racing, replete with timely tips on how to handle a variety of skiing situations that may require special mental and physical skills.

The book focuses on high-performance fundamentals in chapters 1 to 4 and on high-performance skills in chapters 5 to 9. Each chapter concludes with a summary of the material covered in the chapter. You might find reading the summary first to be an interesting way to begin a chapter.

Chapter 1 is an exploration of high-performance skiing: How do you measure high performance, and how do you assess your ability? We jump right into high-performance equipment in chapter 2, where we discuss ski shape and construction, ski tuning, and selecting clothing and equipment. In chapter 3 we discuss progressive principles of training (we are passionate about this stuff), including warming up and cooling down, the five training seasons, physical conditioning, strength building, flexibility training, the value of rest, and the importance of fluid intake. If you run, cycle, in-line skate, rock climb, hike, swim, kayak, play tennis or racquetball, play soccer, or take part in triathlons or other athletic activities in addition to skiing, you'll find this chapter an ideal approach to your year-round training for glory.

Chapter 4 is a step-by-step strategy for getting ready for aggressive, fun-filled, injury-free skiing in a variety of common snow conditions. Also provided is a strategy for getting the most out of your first day of skiing for the new season. Though the tendency is to forget advice on tips for the first day of the season (because you're in a hurry to make those first turns and charge into your ski season), we urge you to take a look at this section. You might pick up some tips and some easy-to-accommodate ideas that may actually add to your enjoyment of and performance on that first day out.

The book kicks into high gear with chapters 5, 6, and 7, where we discuss and illustrate steep-slope skiing, mastering the moguls, and the thrill of powder. In each of these chapters we discuss essential strategy and technique, high-performance skills, and, as appropriate, special situations and performance tips.

In chapters 8 and 9 we dig deeply into contemporary racing and on-snow training, illustrating the dynamic aspects of training for and competing in ski racing. In chapter 8 you'll find racing essentials, high-performance racing skills, tips on mental preparation, and, of course, your introduction to the world of on-snow race training drills and exercises. Novice and recreational racers as well as training-hungry veterans will find this chapter useful. Hopefully our racing tips and encouragement will be all you need to don a racing bib this winter.

In chapter 9 we focus on improving your skiing by honing your overall skills and slope sense. Reading conditions and slopes, identifying common faults in your ski technique, and skill improvement drills are all discussed and illustrated. The chapter closes with important tips on how to use ski school classes to improve your overall skiing experience.

It will forever remain true that there is no one way to ski correctly. Skiing is as individual as our signatures. Common to all skiers, however, are a number of skills, strategies, concepts, and techniques that each of us interprets in a way best suited to our body type, flexibility, athletic aptitude, physical conditioning, and overall sports attitude.

In all performance sports, athletes must be realistic and honest with themselves, particularly when pursuing skill sports such as skiing. Skill development takes time; rushing it leads to frustration, unrealistic personal demands, and often injury. If you don't try to ski like anyone but yourself and take a patient, yet purposeful, approach to high-performance skiing, you'll enjoy your interpretation of the concepts in this book. Getting better in sports doesn't have to mean all work and no play. In fact, for recreational sports the equation is probably best stated as "mostly play, some work." You choose the balance of play and work; we will give you the tools.

John Yacenda

ACKNOWLEDGMENTS

The second edition of *High-Performance Skiing* wouldn't be possible if Martin Barnard hadn't worked so tirelessly to pull together the early elements of the writing of it. And this book wouldn't be what it is today without the dedication and team spirit inspired by Marni Basic. To both of them, I am grateful and appreciative.

J.Y.

Werner Margreiter, my mentor in skiing and coaching. Current and former U.S. Ski Team coaches Georg Capaul, Bill Egan, Thor Kallerud, and Keven Burnett for their constant willingness to share knowledge. Ron Kipp and Lester Keller who are always interested in brainstorming on skiing. Shawn Smith, PSIA Demonstration Team Captain, for his help over the years in current ski teaching.

T.R.

Our photograph models Rob Sogard, PSIA Demonstration Team member; Barbara Sanders, Supervisor, Mammoth Mountain Ski School; and Rob Clayton, Coach, Park City Ski Education Foundation; for their enthusiasm and technical expertise. Mammoth Mountain Ski Area.

CHAPTER 1

THE HIGH-PERFORMANCE SKIER

Skiing at its most basic level challenges you to think about what you need to do on your skis and go out on the slopes to do it. Then, as the stakes get higher, you need to know more and be able to express this knowledge on skis, in the bumps and powder, on ice, in the race course, in crud, in the steeps, and elsewhere over the span of mountainous snow-covered terrain. In this book we assume that you already ski and have a love or curiosity for the sport, and that you want to learn how to become a high-performance skier.

The basics of high-performance skiing are a blend of technical skills, physical attitude, powers of the mind, and awareness of your capabilities. In the chapters that follow, we will show you how to hone your technical skills in almost any skiing situation while fine-tuning your physical attitude. We will also explore both the intellectual and the emotional aspects of high-performance skiing.

1. **Technical skills** include being balanced over your skis with independent legs and skis; having a muscularly relaxed stance; being versatile in different kinds of turns and the linking of these turns; having edge control in varied conditions; controlling speed (acceleration and deceleration); using poles

appropriately; moving efficiently; being versatile in using the whole length of the ski as well as the inside and outside edges; and relying on keen ski–snow sensitivity, called *ski feel.*

2. **Physical attitude** includes being reactional: sometimes fearless and aggressive as you work your skis; sometimes loose and light with little pressure on your skis as they ride or glide atop the snow and few inappropriate contractions of your muscles; and sometimes playful and adventurous.

3. **Mental powers** include having confidence, followed by a sense of pride and accomplishment; being able to set goals; having determination, inner direction, an acceptance of personal growth, and the desire to learn; controlling the fear of failure; and having a respect for other skiers, boarders, and the mountain itself.

By chapter 5, after discussions of equipment, conditioning, and snow conditions, you'll be skiing the steeps and jumping off cornices; in subsequent chapters we'll take you skiing in moguls, powder, the race course, crud, slush, and more. High-performance skiers ski at all levels and in all conditions. You needn't be an Olympic racer or expert skier to ski at a high-level of performance. Rather, you have only to pursue high performance in all levels of skiing, be it your 5th or 500th time through the race course, mogul field, or trees. Unless you appreciate the fundamentals of every step toward a higher level of performance, you may be disappointed with your lack of progress, even though you're trying hard to improve.

Regardless of whether you're an intermediate, advanced intermediate, expert, or super expert skier, there is always that hill, mountain, or mogul run that presents difficulty. If you perceive difficulty with a slope or condition, you will experience difficulty; you will have reinforced the difficulty with the power of your mind.

ARE YOU A HIGH-PERFORMANCE SKIER?

One of the most direct—and subjective—methods to find out if skiers are really advancing to high-performance skiing is to test their skills and confidence on those slopes or under those conditions that intimidated them. Although this can help one's skiing, it can also reinforce counterproductive habits. Ask yourself five questions about your skiing:

1. Are you relaxed mentally and physically?
2. Do you feel confident with your turns?
3. Are you able to make subtle adjustments of speed without making erratic moves?
4. Do you keep your attention focused downhill, skiing the fall line without hesitation?
5. Do you experience the feeling of effortless control as you move your skis in a pendulum-type way, reaching out side to side beneath you, moving your weight from ski to ski while skiing an efficient line down the mountain (see figure 1.1)?

If you answered "yes" to all of these questions, you are a high-performance skier. If you answered "no" or "sometimes" to some of the questions, the information in this book should help you improve your skiing so that eventually you can answer "yes" to all of them, regardless of the slope and snow conditions.

Figure 1.1 Floating and steering the inside ski ("effortless control").

HIGH PERFORMANCE BY THE EXPERTS

You might find it amusing or embarrassing that teachers and coaches can know your level of performance simply by watching certain aspects of your skiing. Christin Cooper, 1982 World Championship triple medalist (silver in slalom, silver in giant slalom, and bronze in combined), 1984 Olympic Silver Medalist in the giant slalom, Skiing Hall of Fame member, and television commentator, gave us her impressions of high-performance skiers coming down the mountain. "They're really solid on their skis, and dynamic. They work from ski to ski while playing with the terrain and remaining relaxed. Their basic position is balanced over the middle of their skis. This provides the control without the risk of their skis getting away from them." She concluded, "You can tell when skiers have a lot of miles behind their skiing, and when these miles have included a lot of disciplined training doing the basics."

KEY TRAITS OF HIGH-PERFORMANCE SKIERS

High-performance skiers have three traits that enable them to both get the maximum from their sense of the snow and mountain and know the best way to ski in many situations: confidence, ability to ski reactionally, and ski feel. These traits are the basis of a skier's emotional, athletic, and sensory approaches to the sport.

Confidence

Confidence allows the high-performance skier to remain relaxed until the last turn or the last gate in a race course. Confidence is built on plenty of exposure to powder, the steeps, the bumps, or racing. As skiers develop confidence, they acquire versatility and a dynamic attitude about skiing. They are able to relax or ski aggressively depending on the conditions.

High-performance skiing is an evolutionary development that each skier goes through at his or her own pace. If you think like a high-performance skier early in your skiing, you will ski with more purpose and dedication. With this sense of purpose, you can progress rapidly to the point where the changes in your skiing are subtle and small. It is at this point in your skiing when the perfection of skills takes place: the refinement of your skiing in varied and difficult snow conditions. Through this development you become *reactional* and *instinctive* in your skiing, no longer needing to think about what you're doing.

Reactional and Instinctive Skiing

To ski reactionally and move instinctively to changes in conditions and skill demands, take the thought out of your skiing and go with the flow of the terrain. The curse of putting too much thought in your skiing is to become overfocused on one aspect to the extent that you forget about other aspects and end up fighting with balance. Too often, skiers fight the conditions and attempt to overcome out-of-balance situations or momentary acceleration by bracing themselves against the environment as opposed to flowing with it. When you start down any hill you want to feel that the terrain is doing the work for you, the skis are doing the work they are designed to do, and you are enjoying the ride.

With drills, exercises, and time on skis you can learn to ski *reactionally,* that is, make a very quick read of the terrain. If it is crusty, cruddy, icy, bumpy, or poorly lit, don't panic—react. Your skills are combined with your sense of how you want to ski this condition. When you react and respond to the condition, the skis work for you, and energy expenditure is minimal. You can feel the skis do more of the work. In effect, the conditions help you ski at a high level.

Skiing reactionally means never being static. You flow with the changes in terrain, and your upper body is quiet and still while your legs do the work. As you keep your upper body relaxed and headed down the fall line, your lower body moves by reacting to the cues it receives from the terrain and relays to your brain. The brain instantaneously interprets the sensory information that it receives from your hands, face, ears, inner ears, eyes, and feet. When you ski reactionally, you are efficient and ready to attack any situation for which you have the skills—and you're likely smiling.

If the skills are there, it is self-confidence that allows skiers to be relaxed and aggressive in any situation. Skiers are confident when they start down the hill, and often have a mental picture of how they are going to ski the hill. This image is so vivid, skiers can almost feel the run before they ski it. Once their skills are developed, skiers know they can do with their skis what they imagine in their minds. Confidence, perception, and imagery allow skiers to be aggressive and know that they can adjust to any changes in conditions. This mind-set lets skiers stay in balance while in motion, which is critical to versatile skiing.

Ski Feel

High-performance skiers have keen ski–snow sensitivity called *ski feel*. They have the skills to respond to their perception of how to ski a particular run and feel relaxed doing it. Skiers who are not relaxed in the race course can't function well. Compared to high-performance skiers, first-timers do not feel the snow and the terrain. They are inhibited, working against feeling; their skiing is cerebral, which creates physical rigidity. Skiers who have developed ski feel seem to float down the hill.

Ski feel is a concept like balance, which is instinctual to some people but can also be learned. Ski feel can be developed through any sport that combines angles of balance and the sensitivity of pressure from an outside force, either gravity or the resistance of water, ice, ground, or snow. Running is an example of such a sport. Through the runner's shoes, the feet and toes identify the terrain and send messages to the brain that the ground is either soft, hard, slippery, or rocky. These sensations allow for adjustments to balance and stride length.

High-performance skiers have developed ski feel and ski–snow awareness from years of skiing and thinking about the sport. These skiers instinctively know when to use or release pressure on their skis, and when to angle their ankles, knees, hips, or shoulders to create or relax the edging of their skis. Their sense of the snow comes from time spent experiencing the different feelings and pressures of their skis on various snow surfaces.

Overall, when you think about ski feel, think sensory:

- *Sight.* Look at the snow and conditions.
- *Sound.* The sound of your skis against the snow reveals much about the conditions and your mastery of skiing skills.
- *Touch.* Feel the texture of the snow with your hands and feet.
- *Balance.* Recognize that the more relaxed and confidently you ski, the more your balance helps to correct any ill-chosen reactions to unexpected snow conditions or poorly executed moves. The result is that you fall less often after making clumsy maneuvers.

PATIENCE AND FITNESS

Skiers' goals must be complemented by a willingness to go through the process of skill development. Two important factors in this development are patience and fitness. If skiers are patient, their learning process can take its natural course; if skiers are fit and in skier tone (cardiovascular fitness along with strength and flexibility), they will have the stamina to persevere with practice. Patience and fitness make it easy to develop a healthy mental attitude to complement your physical willingness.

Skiers for whom an aggressive mental attitude overwhelms physical capabilities may find frustration. Likewise, skiers who are physically strong yet haven't the attitude to work toward goals will be frustrated with their progress. The best approach is to blend mental desires and physical capabilities, thereby allowing the development of skiing skills through experience and exposure.

TYPES OF SKIERS

Many children use *skeletal bracing* when they first start skiing. Children skiing in a wedge or snowplow position seem to be hinged back, their legs straight and bodies bent at the waist. They are braced. Instructors, parents, and friends encourage the children to bend their ankles and knees, but due to their immature muscular development, children need to use structural rather than muscular strength. Children are using their skeletal strength when their legs are straight, bracing against the skis and the snow.

Adults often stop using skeletal bracing. Skeletal bracing is a skill that, when used properly, allows for efficient skiing. Skiers who don't occasionally rely on skeletal bracing tax their muscle strength unnecessarily. Skiers who stand up, keep themselves tall, and use angles from their shoulders to their hips, knees, and ankles, ski more efficiently. You can create angles throughout the skeletal structure (see figure 1.2, a and b).

Using these angles lessens the amount of muscle support needed to hold any one position or any series of positions.

Mike Iman, master teacher, highly respected ski school director and accomplished skier and racer, is fond of saying that there are essentially three types of recreational skiers with respect to muscles, skills, and skeletal bracing: the inefficient skier, the efficient but tricky skier, and the disciplined, athletic skier.

Figure 1.2, a and b Skeletal bracing throughout the turn conserves muscle energy.

The Inefficient Skier

Inefficient skiers tend to become fatigued by two o'clock in the afternoon. This is due to a lack of physical conditioning and a lack of efficiency (i.e., the overuse of muscle and movement). Instead of using skeletal bracing, or standing tall, and allowing outside influences to help work with the skis, the inefficient skier frequently muscles the ski around the mountain, expending too much energy and tiring quickly. The result is often muscle soreness, strains, or more serious joint and bone injuries.

The Efficient but Tricky Skier

These skiers are at the midpoint in skills acquisition, mental perspective, and physical attitude. They ski technically well and, due to their sound physical conditioning, with a blend of muscular control and skeletal bracing along with a collection of technically sneaky tricks. They have an inborn ability to stay in balance and their movement patterns seem very precise. They look very smooth, yet do not really espouse high-performance skills. One of the most common "sneaky tricks" is prematurely lifting the inside ski and "sneaking" it next to the outside ski to effect a parallel turn, thus avoiding the technical discipline to keep the inside ski on the snow as it is smoothly steered to initiate a parallel turn. Another is the "shoulder pole-plant"—that is, the dipping of the shoulder to initiate a turning sequence instead of using a full or partial pole swing motion preceding the pole-plant or touch.

The Disciplined, Athletic Skier

This skier knows how to ski proficiently. The disciplined, athletic skier is a high-performance mover: technically sound, physically fit, aggressive, confident, and committed to skiing and off-season training (see figure 1.3).

BLOCKS TO BECOMING A HIGH-PERFORMANCE SKIER

Tentativeness and avoiding new skiing experiences may keep a very good recreational skier from becoming a high-performance skier.

Figure 1.3 Completing a dynamic curve.

This skier may choose to ski powder only when it is very light and four to five inches deep, or only small, developing moguls when the lighting is good and there is no real hard pack or ice. This skier prefers the familiar; new situations are often dismissed as too difficult. Because the skier avoids new challenges, he or she may become stagnant and miss the opportunity for greater skiing potential. It is important to try new situations. Ski the runs that trouble you; ski them the best you can.

At first, it may seem like you are skiing more awkwardly and inefficiently than properly. If you keep trying the new runs as many times as you ski the familiar ones, eventually the new runs will become your forte; if you continue to add different runs, conditions, and situations to your skiing, you will break out of your tentativeness. If you avoid the challenges, however, you are likely to stay in a rut that keeps you from becoming a high-performance skier.

Infrequent skiing is another obstacle to the development of high-performance skills. Good recreational skiers may be able to go skiing only a few days in a season, leading to hesitation and ambivalence.

THE MYTH OF THE PERFECTLY CARVED TURN

There is no such thing as a perfectly carved turn, except in reference to a turn with a very long radius. It would take an entire run to make that single turn. There is, however, a relatively perfect, carved turn: There is a subtle, continuous, and patient steering of the inside ski, and a patient foot-guiding of the turning (outside) ski onto its edge until a certain point when it is time to get off that edge, to minimize skidding, and onto the other ski.

a   *(continued)*

Figure 1.4, a-c Carved turn—skier emphasizing inside ski steering while applying pressure and edge control to both skis, and patiently steering both skis to finish the turn.

Figure 1.4, a-c
(continued)

We teach beginning and intermediate skiers to make *skidded turns* to help control their speed and turn. In a skidded turn, the skier emphasizes rotary, rapid steering first, then pressures the downhill or outside ski, and finally uses the edges of the skis to control movement or speed. As skiers advance to higher levels of skiing, they abandon skidded turns and embrace the dynamics of carved turns. In carved turns, skiers emphasize inside ski steering while applying pressure and edge control to both skis (see figure 1.4, a-c); they finish the turn using rotary motion or ski steering (constant steering with both inside and outside skis).

With carved turns, the inside (uphill) ski has to be constantly moving away from the turning ski to effect a truly carved turn. There are many levels of carved turning you can create with inside-ski steering:

- You can accomplish beginning carving with your downhill ski by lightening the inside ski, relaxing the pressure of your leg or foot, and letting the ski glide atop the snow rather than through it.

- To accomplish more advanced carving with your downhill ski, steer the lightened inside ski away from the turning ski, directing the knee of this inside leg uphill (see figure 1.5, a-d).

- Achieve extreme carving with your downhill ski by diverging the inside ski away from the turning ski, radically pushing off of your downhill ski, and directing or stepping the inside ski diagonally uphill to the inside of the turn (see figure 1.6, a-c).

Whether or not your turns are carved, and to what degree, says a lot about your level of performance. The new hourglass ski design has improved skiers' turning, especially the development of carved turns. Nevertheless, skiers must still apply basic steering and carving skills to maximize their potential for carved turns in myriad situations.

a

b   *(continued)*

Figure 1.5, a-d Advanced carving—steering the lightened inside ski away from the turning ski, directing the knee of the inside leg uphill.

c

Figure 1.5, a-d *(continued)*

a

b

Figure 1.6, a-c Extreme carving—dynamic divergence of inside ski leads to greater carving.

c

Figure 1.6, a-c *(continued)*

KEYS TO HIGH PERFORMANCE

1. Taking the time to learn the fundamentals of skiing will help you progress rapidly and painlessly to the point of consistent performance in your skiing.
2. High-performance skiers blend technical skills, physical attitude, mental powers, and a mastery of changing fall lines.
3. High-performance skiers are dynamic and solid on their skis. They work from ski to ski while playing with the terrain and remaining relaxed. Their basic bodily stance is balanced over the middle of their skis.
4. The perception of difficulty with a slope or condition is a self-fulfilling prophecy; the mind reinforces the difficulty.

5. Confidence is built by experience in a variety of conditions. As confidence develops, so too does versatility and a dynamic attitude about skiing.

6. High-performance skiers have a keen ski–snow sensitivity: ski feel. They have the skills to respond to their perception of how to ski a particular run while remaining relaxed. When thinking about ski feel, think sensory: sight, sound, touch, and sense of balance. Look at the snow, listen to the sound of your skis moving across the snow, be aware of the sensations you receive through your skis and poles to your boots and hands, and relax to be able to respond to balance-threatening situations.

7. Too much thought may cause overfocusing on one aspect of skiing at the expense of other aspects, culminating in a fight with balance.

8. When skiing reactionally and instinctively, a skier responds to changing conditions, never skiing in a static position.

9. The high-performance skier is technically sound, physically fit, aggressive on the slopes, confident, and committed to skiing and off-season training.

10. Tentativeness and the avoidance of new skiing experiences can keep a recreational skier from becoming a high-performance skier.

11. The carve of a turn is influenced by the action of your inside ski, whether it's lightened, steered, or diverged away from your turning ski.

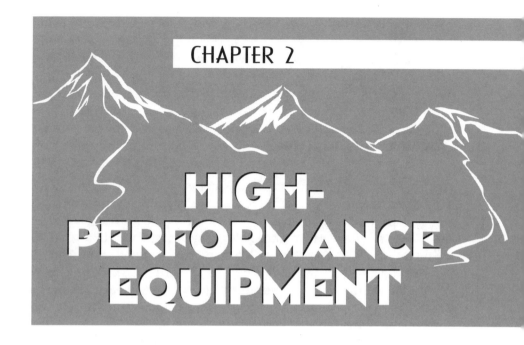

CHAPTER 2

HIGH-PERFORMANCE EQUIPMENT

High-performance skiing is an equipment-intensive sport. Function, fit, and comfort make the difference between success and failure, pleasure and agony. The selection of equipment depends on climate, environment, and, most important, the type of high-performance skiing you wish to do. In this chapter we will guide you through clothing and equipment selection and maintenance to help you reach your high-performance skiing goals.

CLOTHING

High-performance skiers find that the proper selection of clothing is essential for comfort and skiing pleasure. A dream day of cold, crisp, clear air and 18 inches of uncut powder will turn into your worst nightmare after skiing for 45 minutes in your jeans and flannel shirt. Or try hiking for 20 minutes in your insulated snowmobile suit from Sam's Army Navy Discount Store to that secret chute you have always heard about. You will quickly realize that the hot tub on the deck is as damp as the built-in sauna you are wearing.

Today's ski clothing is designed for fit and function. Layering, breathability, venting, and wicking are factors incorporated into products to keep you dry, warm, and comfortable in all snow and weather conditions. Shop for ski clothing at a specialty ski shop and ask a lot of questions about the design and fabrics of the clothing. With the correct clothing you will stay warm and not miss any of the high-performance skiing you desire.

Socks and Underwear

Socks and underwear are important for functional high-performance skiing because they are the garments that come in contact with your skin; they form the foundation for everything else you put on.

It is important to wear undergarments designed for winter athletic activities. In high-performance skiing activities, you will sweat. To maintain skiing comfort in cold or warm weather you need to remove the moisture from your body and clothing. Your undergarments, including socks, long underwear, and long-sleeved T-shirts, should be made of fabric that wicks moisture away from the skin to the outside of the fabric where it can evaporate.

Some underwear fabric has the added feature of hollow-core fibers. This fabric provides extra warmth without extra weight. These products are good for very cold weather skiing or people bothered by the cold.

Look for ski socks that have a double layer of wicking material or an inner layer of wicking material and an outer layer of cotton. These socks will help keep feet warm on a cold day. Most cold feet are a result of damp, sweaty socks.

Intermediate Layers

In recent years, an entire line of ski clothing has been developed using synthetic fleece. This fabric allows the body to breath and lets body moisture escape. The fabric has tiny air pockets that provide insulation. Synthetic fleece wicks perspiration while providing excellent warmth. Also available are fleece and pile with waterproof and wind-resistant properties. Vests, sweaters, pullovers, jackets, and pants of these fabrics serve as intermediate layers on cold days and outerwear for spring skiing.

Outerwear

The outer layer of high-performance clothing must be windproof, water-resistant, breathable, able to be vented, and it must allow body vapor to escape. It also needs to be easy to move in and functional. In some parts of the country, the material will need to be waterproof. Outerwear for high-performance skiing needs to keep you warm on chairlifts, keep the snow out, allow for venting of body vapor and changes in body heat, and be functional in a variety of weather and snow conditions.

The options in outerwear are a jacket and pants or bib, or a one-piece suit. There are advantages and disadvantages of both. Your decision may be based on the climate in which you do most of your skiing and the types of skiing you do.

A one-piece ski suit is good for cold weather. You can change the layers underneath during the day or from day to day. On very cold days, you can add a vest or jacket over the one-piece. One-piece ski suits hold in warm air. Suits are preferable for stormy weather or powder skiing because they have fewer openings for snow to creep in. Suits with little or no insulation can be excellent for spring skiing or warmer climates.

The jacket and pants or bib combination allows for more versatility in a wide range of weather conditions. Skiers can shed the jacket when the weather is warm. Pants can be insulated or not. Bibs provide more warmth around the torso and back than do waist-high pants. Keeping the lower back warm during skiing helps maintain flexibility and prevents stiff back muscles at the end of a long day. Bibs also offer more protection than pants on deep powder days.

These outerwear features are valuable:

- Underarm zippers are the quickest way to control body heat. Use these zippered vents to keep warm on the chairlift or to keep cooler and drier on that 10-minute hike to the back bowls.
- Vent panels across the back of some jackets can be opened or closed to regulate body heat.
- Built-in hoods that fold into a collar are handy when the weather suddenly turns bad.
- Lots of zippered pockets encourage self-sufficiency for the day.
- Inner pockets help keep items dry and warm. (Have you ever tried to eat a frozen candy bar on the chairlift?)
- Two-way zippers assist in function and minute adjustments of body heat.
- Waist drawcords can help regulate body heat.

Gloves

Cold fingers can ruin an otherwise great day. Waterproof gloves are the most functional hand protection for high-level skiing. Mittens may keep your hands warmer, but make it harder to hold poles, handle zippers, and adjust boots. Look for the standard features of gloves: a combination of waterproof fabric, leather palm and finger pads, and an insulated lining. A wrist cuff to fill the gap between the body of the glove and jacket sleeve keeps snow out and warmth in. Lightweight gloves are appropriate for warm days. Some companies offer zip-in liners for quicker drying or for wearing alone in warm weather.

BOOTS

Boots may be your most important investment. Poorly fitting boots mean less than optimal performance. The high-performance skier wants the boots to fit so well that when he or she steps into the bindings, the skis seem to be as rigidly attached to the legs as are the feet.

Think of the boots as gaskets connecting your feet to your skis. Various devices in boots provide flex, cant your foot, lift your heel, advance your forward lean, stabilize your arch, and so on. But first the boot must fit properly.

Buying Boots

When buying boots, use a reputable ski shop or specialty boot shop to help you properly select and fit the boots. Make sure you purchase the ideal boots for your own high-performance skiing. When shopping for boots, follow these tips:

1. Spend some time talking to the shop's boot-fitting expert. Every ski boot manufacturer has a full line of boots from entry level to high-end racing boots. Have the expert review a variety of boots.

2. Give the expert an honest assessment of your technical skiing level and the type of skiing that most interests you. Some people try to impress shop employees with their skiing proficiency and then end up with equipment that does not meet their needs.

3. Try on boots while wearing the socks you will use for skiing.

4. Try on boots from different manufacturers and from within one manufacturer's line. This will give you comparisons on fit, flex, and

comfort. Size and shape will vary between companies because each company works from its own set of lasts, formed shapes or molds of the human foot. You will find variations in length, width, and shape of the foot space in different boots. For your comfort and function, it is important to select the boot with the best possible fit to your foot.

5. To find the general size needed for you, take the liner out of one of the boots and put your foot into the shell. Move your foot forward until your toes just touch the front of the shell. If there is space for about two fingers between your heel and the back of the shell, you should be close to the correct size.

6. Stand up straight; your toes should not have a great deal of room, but should not touch the front of the boot. If you can't wiggle your toes, the boot is too small.

7. The heel pocket is one of the critical areas in boot fit. It is important for the heel pocket of the boot to hold your heel snugly in place. Fasten the buckles and try to lift your heel within the boot. If you can, the boot is too big. Your heel must be held firmly in place without being uncomfortable.

8. Even if a boot fits in width and length, it may not fit at the calf. When buckled, the top of the boot must not constrict the calf. After fastening the buckles, press your shin forward and see if you can slip two fingers into the boot behind your leg. If you can't, the boot may be too small; if the space is too great the boot may be too big.

9. Wear the boots in the shop for at least 20 to 30 minutes. After this time, the boot must still fit very snugly. Boots will stretch a half to a full size after a few days of skiing due to the movement of the material in the lining. In high-performance skiing, your boots become your ankles and feet. A tight-fitting boot at purchase will become a well-fitting boot when used.

Boot Flex and Modifications

For the high-performance skier to maintain balance, the ankles must flex when the knees do. Therefore, boots that are too stiff will not allow you to ski in optimal balance. The boots should be stiff enough to provide you with good lateral and fore/aft support and yet soft enough to allow ankle flexion when you bend your knees. When trying on boots in the warm ski shop, keep in mind that materials in the boot stiffen in cold weather, making the boot harder to flex. Many people buy top of the line boots and then find the model is too stiff for their strength and skiing abilities. Find the boot that works best for you.

Modern boots may offer a wide range of features such as internal canting of the foot or leg shaft, forward lean adjustment, and heel height adjustments. It is not mandatory to have these features in your boots, but if you do, take time to use each feature. Experiment with settings and adjustments to find what is best for your skiing. Many ski schools offer programs where you can work with an instructor and ski shop experimenting with your boot adjustments to fit your skiing style and technique. A day with experts both in skiing and boot adjustments may be just the thing you need to move into high-performance skiing.

Foot beds or orthotics can be valuable for comfort and to maximize fit. Boots are made from common lasts; these devices compensate for individual differences in foot size, shape, and structure. They place each foot in a correct anatomical position in the ski boot, allowing the foot and ankle to function properly. A specialty ski shop will be able to assist you with foot beds or orthotics.

Whether you have new boots or are using old ones, you may need to have the boots modified. A quality ski shop boot mechanic can improve the fit and function of your boots in several ways, including padding for a better fit, expanding an area of the boot to fit a foot anomaly, softening the flex, canting (adjusting laterally) the cuff, or adding heel lifts. Any of these procedures can dramatically improve your skiing performance.

Boot Maintenance

There are two items to add to your ski locker to help maintain your boots. CatTracts are polyethylene devices that fit over the sole of your ski boots for walking. Not only do CatTracts improve traction, but, more importantly, they save wear and tear on your boot soles, extending the life of your boots. When skiing, they fit easily into a jacket pocket. A compact, inexpensive, electric boot dryer is a must for warm skiing on consecutive days. Buy a brand that uses cool or warm air. A hot air dryer can damage bootliners, insoles, or foot beds. Most ski shops have these products.

BINDINGS

Ski bindings are designed solely for your skiing safety. Bindings keep your boots attached to the skis most of the time, but are designed to release your boots from the skis when forces become great enough to cause injury to bones, joints, or muscles. Considering the speed, pressures, and forces that come into play, bindings serve a very important purpose.

Each binding has a range of settings or adjustments called the DIN (Deutsche Industrial Norm) setting. There are charts that calculate the DIN setting for every skier. The DIN setting is based on the skier's height, weight, skiing ability (one, two, or three), age (only if fifty or older), and ski boot sole length, and indicates how the bindings need to be set for maximum safety and performance. Once a ski shop binding mechanic has used the chart to calculate your DIN setting, you should maintain that setting. If the DIN setting is too low, you risk premature binding release, which can lead to unnecessary falls. If the DIN setting is too high, the binding may not release in a fall, possibly resulting in injury.

Buy bindings only from a reputable ski shop. It is not a good idea to buy secondhand bindings. Each model of bindings has a range of DIN settings. A child's binding may range from 1 to 4; a racing binding may have a range of 8 to 16. When buying bindings, select a model that would put your DIN setting in the middle of the range. For example, if your DIN setting from the charts is 8, a good binding for you would have a DIN range of 4 to 12. This will ensure that the bindings operate to their optimum efficiency.

Check the DIN setting on your skis often to make sure that it is where it should be. Keep bindings clean and free of dirt, road grime, or salt from spring or summer skiing. If you transport your skis on a car roof rack, use a ski bag or keep the bindings covered. At least yearly, have a ski shop check your bindings to assure proper operation.

POLES

Poles are easy to select. Proper pole length is important for maintaining a good, balanced stance and a quiet upper body. To determine proper pole length, stand in your ski boots with the pole turned over so the tip is facing up. Grab the pole directly under the basket with the hand in a normal position. If the pole is the correct length, your forearm will be parallel with the ground.

Always ski with your pole straps around your wrist. This will keep you from accidentally dropping your pole or having it knocked out of your hand. If you lose a pole basket, replace it immediately. Skiing without a basket disrupts technique because you cannot control the depth of the pole in the snow. A pole without a basket can also be unsafe.

SKIS

You are ready for high-performance skiing. There are exciting and challenging adventures awaiting you in the many realms of alpine skiing. You may find yourself becoming a powder hound, a master of the moguls, an aspiring racer, a cruiser, or an extreme skier, challenging the steeps, chutes, and cornices. Regardless of your specialty, you will rely on the main tools of the trade, your high-performance skis.

Ski designers today offer specialty skis for any avenue you wish to take. Before you select the ski type or size that is best for you, it is important to understand why a ski is designed the way it is, how a ski is constructed, and what the ski can do for you.

Ski Design Features

If you know what the design features of skis are and how they work, you will be able to use your skis more effectively. Also, you will be able to select skis that complement your own style of high-performance skiing. Four components of ski design separate a $500 pair of high-performance skis from two six-foot-long two-by-four boards, which sell for under $5 (see figure 2.1):

- **Flex** is the ability of a ski to bend. A soft-flex ski bends easily and is designed for a lighter skier. A stiff flex in a ski requires either more body weight to bend the ski or a more aggressive skier.
- **Sidecut** is the difference in width between the waist (middle) of the ski and the tip and tail. Sidecut and flex are extremely important to efficiency in high-performance skiing.
- **Camber** is the bend or bow of a ski. It is camber that distributes the weight of the skier along the length of the ski.

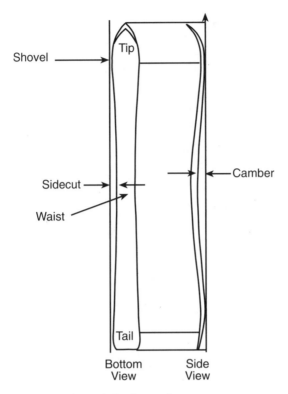

Figure 2.1 Parts of a ski and ski design features.

- **Torsional rigidity** keeps a ski from twisting along its longitudinal axis.

High-performance skiers rely heavily on their skis just as carpenters, mechanics, and surgeons rely on their tools. The flex, sidecut, camber, and length of your skis, together with your technical skills, influence the behavior of the skis (for example, how they turn or carve) on the snow.

The relationship between ski geometry and construction, edge angle, and pressure distribution are key factors influencing the turning of the ski. A pressurized and edged ski develops a reverse bend (reverse camber) and forms an arc against the snow. The radius of the arc depends on the sidecut of the ski, the amount of pressure the ski exerts against the snow, and the edge angle of the ski (how far it is tipped up on edge). As the ski moves forward in the snow with the reverse camber and edge angle, the ski produces a clean track, where the tail of the ski follows the same path as the tip. This is a

Figure 2.2 Types of skis for high-performance skiing. Left to right: giant slalom ski, slalom ski, "fat boy" powder ski, shaped ski, and super sidecut ski.

carving turn. It shows the influence of skiing technique on design: form follows function.

Carving a turn is important to a racer. However, there are other types of high-performance skiing (skiing the steeps, mastering the moguls, challenging the thrill of powder, and all-mountain cruising). Selecting skis to maximize performance is extremely important (see figure 2.2).

Ski Selection

When evaluating equipment it is important to study the design features, determine how these features affect skiing, and then decide if you want that effect in your skiing. Ski manufacturers have designed lines of skis to meet the needs of all types of skiers. The components that vary the most in ski design, and on which the various categories of high-performance skiing depend, are length, flex, and sidecut.

Shaped Skis. Ski manufacturers today are doing creative designwork in the area of sidecut of skis. This has led to a line of skis called *shaped skis*. The Professional Ski Instructors of America define shaped skis as those with an hourglass appearance: wide tips and tails but narrow under the foot. The hourglass shape varies from manufacturer to manufacturer. Because of this variance, there is a range of tasks that shaped skis can and cannot perform. In the next section we comment on when shaped skis are and are not beneficial.

Sidecut of a ski is the biggest factor in the efficiency of turn size and shape. The greater the degree of sidecut in relation to the length of the ski, the shorter, smaller turn a ski will carve. An extreme sidecut allows a ski to carve turns with more ease than a conventional sidecut. With shaped skis, an intermediate skier can explore the movements of advanced skiing. He or she can discover how to carve turns with body angulation and pressure on the ski. Shaped skis, especially the super sidecut ones, are great learning tools in the zone of discovery between intermediate and advanced skiing—they will allow a skier to advance quickly into parallel ski turns. A super sidecut ski can help you master carved, parallel turns by helping you learn skill-based movements that you can then apply to carved turns on more conventional skis.

Super sidecut skis have limited use for conventional all-mountain skiing. However, many people enjoy them using a skiing technique similar to snowboarding. By using full-body inclination, the skier makes clean, carved turns in all types of terrain. Some of these skiers use ski poles, while others do not. When watching from a distance it is hard to tell if the skier is on shaped skis or a snowboard. This is an area you may want to explore that might open up a whole new avenue of high-performance skiing.

There is a huge difference in sidecut between a new giant slalom ski compared to one from the early 1990s. Although today's giant slalom ski cannot be defined as shaped, the sidecut is dramatic compared to that of skis of only a few years ago. Conservatively shaped skis will allow you to refine your technical skiing skills while expanding the terrain options that fit into your skiing comfort zone.

Because shaped skis are wider in the tips and tails, the edge length and base surface area are greater than on a conventional ski. For this

Skiing on Shaped Skis

The *shaped ski* is a modern, skier-friendly version of the original, extreme sidecut and shorter parabolic ski introduced by Elan in the early '90s. Even though this so-called hourglass ski has been both praised and criticized, refinements in shaped-ski design have made it a hot item on the slopes. Testament to the popularity of the shaped ski is the fact that most ski areas have invested in shaped skis for their rental departments, with some resorts offering shaped skis as their standard rental. Ironically, skiers at these resorts must request traditionally shaped skis if they don't want the new shaped skis.

Resorts have found through testing and public comments that shaped skis make skier visits more enjoyable: First-day-of-the-season skiers find they have a more fluid (and shorter) reacquaintance period with skiing, skiers like to ski longer, skiers are more inclined to enjoy the terrain and ski experience, and skiers generally feel a revived interest in the sport.

Many resorts offer free or low-cost classes for people using shaped skis, and it's a smart way for skiers to introduce themselves to the dynamics of these skis. Naturally, the big question you might want answered about such lessons is: Will you, a good skier, be taught anything you can immediately translate to your skiing on shaped skis? The answer is: Yes, generally, there are plenty of tips you can pick up to assist you in maximizing the benefits from the different design of these skis. Here are five:

1. Shaped skis are made to turn, but they turn more "quietly" than conventionally shaped skis—that is, you don't need as much rotary lower-leg and foot steering or dramatic edging to guide the skis into and out of turns.

2. To turn shaped skis, you use your lower legs from the knees down to tip the skis on edge, thereby engaging their design (i.e., hourglass shape) to turn.

3. Shaped skis can be skied much more horizontally than conventional skis—that is, you don't need to be as vertical (standing as tall) to flatten the skis before rolling them onto another edge to turn. Instead, you extend your legs to the side as you edge the skis to effect the turn and retract your legs as you move the skis beneath you before extending them to the other side to turn the other way.

4. Overall, you can ski on shaped skis in a more compact stance. Due to the wide shovel (tip) design, having your weight farther forward allows you to engage the ski very early in the turn—and to

→

turn quickly by simply rolling your knees to the right to turn right and to the left to turn left.

5. Shaped skis (which can be 5 to 10 centimeters shorter than your regular skis and still perform well) encourage you to ski with a wider stance and to be more patient with your turns—very important if you roll your knees to turn.

Now some general advice. *Don't believe anything you hear or read about shaped skis until you go out and try them—including my advice.* Different skiers will ski on shaped skis differently; while my five tips are pretty much on target for shaped skis in general, you'll apply these tips variably to fit your style of skiing.

If you're thinking about buying a new pair of skis, consider trying out the shaped ski. Ski resort rental packages are an inexpensive full-day trial; you may want to try several different designs of shaped ski before buying.

I am exuberant about my experience with shaped skis. They skied well in tight turns, medium turns, and high-speed long turns. Surprisingly, they held very steady in a high-speed tuck and did well off jumps and rolls. But one thing became apparent in skiing on the shaped ski: the degree of control and comfort at any speed is directly related to the looseness and quietness of your feet, just as it is on conventional skis.

reason, you should choose shaped skis in a shorter length than conventional skis. Each ski manufacturer has its specific conversions, but most recommend shaped skis 10 to 20 centimeters shorter than conventional skis.

All-Mountain Skis. Today, many companies have an *all-mountain ski*. It is designed for the all-around, advanced skier who likes to explore all conditions and types of skiing. These skis have a medium stiffness with an average sidecut, similar to stiffness and sidecut of a giant slalom racing ski. They should be about 5 to 15 centimeters longer than the skier's height. In the next few paragraphs, we will call this the *conventional ski.* If you prefer to focus on one type of skiing, you may want to look into a more specially designed ski. We will elaborate on some of these specially designed skis using the conventional ski as a reference.

Powder Skis. A powder ski has a soft, consistent flex allowing more bending in soft snow than a conventional ski. It is a wide ski with more surface area which, in deep powder, helps keep the ski on the surface. The skis can be shorter. The length depends on the width since the key component is overall surface area. A popular powder ski today is a type called *fat boys*. These are one and a half times wider than conventional skis; thus their length can match, or be 10 centimeters shorter than, the skier's height.

Recreational Slalom Skis. A recreational slalom ski is good for mogul skiing. It has more sidecut and is shorter (5 centimeters above or below the skier's height) than a conventional ski for quicker turning abilities. The ski should have a soft flex, especially in the tail.

For steep, extreme skiing, select a ski that works in powder but also on hard snow. The ski should be stiffer than a powder ski in order to be more responsive. It should probably have a conventional sidecut with the edges kept sharp. The ski needs to have dampening characteristics like a giant slalom ski in order to absorb vibrations. The length should be similar to a conventional ski.

Slalom and Giant Slalom Skis. For high-performance racing, decide whether to race on one pair of skis or to use both slalom and giant slalom skis. Giant slalom skis have more sidecut than conventional skis and a medium to stiff flex. They perform best in medium radius turns. The skis should have design features to reduce vibration. This will allow the ski to be smooth at high speeds. The normal length is 5 to 15 centimeters above the skier's height. Shaped skis are 10 to 15 centimeters shorter than normal length. If using shaped skis for giant slalom, they should not have an extreme sidecut, but a conservatively shaped profile.

A slalom ski has a stiff flex, especially in the tail. It will have more sidecut than a conventional ski to facilitate quick turning in a short radius. A shaped ski, however, probably has too much sidecut to be used for slalom. Slalom skis are usually constructed of light material to reduce the swing weight of the ski for quicker turning. The ski length will be 0 to 10 centimeters above the skier's height.

If using only one pair of skis for both slalom and giant slalom racing, skier preference dictates whether it is a slalom or giant slalom ski. Experiment with demo skis to find which type works best for you.

When selecting skis for high-performance skiing, take your time and try different skis. Ski companies often have demo days at ski areas so you can try different skis. Most specialty ski shops have demo skis that you can try for a day. Often a shop will apply the rental fee of a demo ski to the purchase price of new skis. When trying demos, use them in the kinds of terrain and conditions that you will be skiing. This is the only way you will know if the skis perform optimally for you.

SKI TUNING

Having your ski edges sharp and the bases clean and waxed for the day's conditions is essential to skiing in variable conditions. Just as a car with bald tires will not perform well in a snowstorm, neither will your skis perform well in conditions for which they are not prepared. A ski with poorly prepared edges is like having a car with two nonfunctioning spark plugs—it may run but not at its peak performance.

Tuned skis are not only for the racer looking for seconds or tenths of seconds. Properly tuned and waxed skis will glide, track smoothly, and carve turns well in all snow conditions, and will hold on hard snow. To experience high-performance skiing you need properly prepared and maintained high-performance equipment. Focus daily attention on

- maintaining the bases,
- having smooth, sharp edges, and
- having skis waxed for the day's conditions.

Specialty ski shops offer ski tuning and waxing services. However, learning to maintain your own skis is more cost effective. Daily or weekly touch-ups keep your skis as finely tuned as a race car. Then your skis are truly high-performance equipment.

Start working on your skis as soon as they come home from the ski shop. New skis have had the bases and edges prepared by machine, but they need hand-tuning for precision. Base material and resins used in manufacturing can shrink as they dry, and the shape of the base may change. Also, as you learn to tune and use your high-performance skis, you will become particular about how you like your skis prepared. You will tune the edges to an exact degree of sharpness. You will know where to dull the tips and tails and what kind of bevel to put on the edges.

Ski Tuning Tools

Specialty ski shops can recommend a beginning set of tools for preparing and maintaining your skis. Ski shop and specialty catalogs sell individual tools and starter kits. Once you understand the function of each tool, the hardware store is a less expensive source of tools for your tuning kit (see figure 2.3). A starter kit should include

- pair of ski vices, for holding ski in place while tuning;
- files, for base and edge work (6- or 8-inch Mill Bast, 10- or 12-inch Mill Bast, or 8-inch Pansar);
- file card, for keeping files clean;
- stones, for polishing edges and repairing small burrs (diamond stone, ceramic stone, or Gummi stone);
- true bar, to determine flatness of bases;
- beveling device(s), for both base-edge beveling and side-edge beveling;
- steel scraper, for preparing bases;
- plastic scraper, for removing excess wax;
- groove cleaner, to remove wax from the base groove (if your ski has one);
- assorted sand paper, for finishing bases;
- brushes, for base and wax preparation (nylon, or copper or brass wire);
- wax iron (specialized ski iron or cheap household model);
- supply of waxes, for a range of temperatures; and
- P-TEX sticks, for base repair.

Base Preparation

The goal in base preparation is to make the base perfectly flat from one edge to the other. The bases of new skis were probably machine-prepared; however, they may not be flat because of changes due to the drying and curing of resins, glues, and internal materials. If the skis are base high, the bases need to be sanded or scraped with a metal scraper. If the bases are edge high, you can use a file to file the edges down (see figure 2.4).

To remove base material, hold a sharpened metal scraper between both thumbs and forefingers and push it along the base in long sweeping movements. The base material will come off in very thin films. Use a true bar to see when the base is flat. When the base is almost flat, finish the job with sandpaper on a sanding block. This

Figure 2.3 Basic tuning tools. A = ski vice, B = wax, C = base bevel guide, D = scraper, E = side bevel guide, F = stones, G = files, H = waxing iron, I = c-clamps, J = brushes.

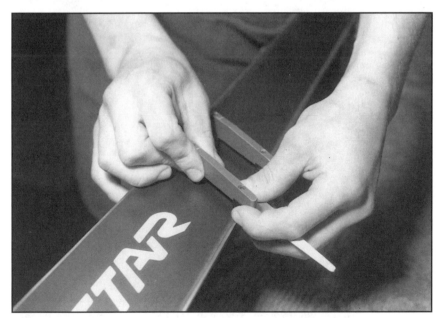

Figure 2.4 Flat filing the bases and base edges of the ski.

will give a fine finish. After the sanding, you can wax the skis and then scrape with a metal scraper to remove some of the remaining rough base fiber (see figure 2.5).

To file the edges, use a 10-inch Mill Bast file held at a 30- to 45-degree angle. With one hand on each end of the file and your thumbs on the file directly over the edges, take long smooth strokes along the base. Use the true bar to see when the edges are flush with the base. Now the base edges are ready for beveling, described in the next section.

If your base material has been damaged, clean the area of all dirt and wax. Select a P-TEX stick the same color as the base material. Light the P-TEX stick with a match or butane torch. Hold the flame close to a metal scraper so the flame burns blue; this will keep carbon from forming. Do not allow the flame to burn red and orange. Heat the stick until you can drip melted P-TEX into the hole or scratch in the base material. Fill the hole above the base level. After the P-TEX has completely cooled, scrape off the excess with a metal scraper; then sand to a fine finish. If the hole or scrape is large, the P-TEX may only last a few days. In this case, have a ski shop place a P-TEX patch into the damaged area.

Figure 2.5 Proper way to hold a scraper for both base scraping and wax removal.

Edge Tuning

Use your thumb and forefinger or the backs of your fingers to feel how sharp your ski edges are. With practice you will become very good at feeling the exact sharpness or dullness of your edges. If you can't feel an edge on your skis that could cut into soft wood, then your edges are probably too rounded and dull to hold in the snow and respond to the subtle movements of your feet and ankles. This distinct edge is necessary for high-performance skiing.

Make sure that the sharpness and smoothness of your edges run the entire length of the ski. When you run your fingers from tip to tail along each edge, it should feel smooth with no rough spots or burrs. Scrape your thumbnail along the ski edge; if the edge peels off a thin film of the nail, the edge is sharp.

Sharpen the edges of the ski from the point of contact with the snow at the tip to the point of contact at the tail. You can determine this point by placing each ski on a flat, smooth surface. Mark the top or side of the ski at the point where each edge comes in contact with the surface. Dull the edges at the tips and tails beyond the contact point: round the edges slightly with a file and then polish the surfaces with a stone. This will keep the skis from hooking, or catching, in the snow. Do not dull the edges that touch the snow or the skis will perform less than optimally.

To tune the edges of the skis, put a slight bevel on both the base edge and the side edge. There are many tools available for edge beveling. Some tools have a specific angle and others have adjustable angles. A shop technician can recommend what to buy. Some of the devices work for both base-edge and side-edge beveling. Others are specifically designed for either base-edge beveling or side-edge beveling; thus you will need two devices.

Putting a bevel on the base edge (see figure 2.6) of the ski allows more accurate and precise turning. A slight bevel on the base edge allows the edge to be engaged quickly when the ski is tilted to initiate a turn. If the ski edge is filed flat, with no base-edge bevel, it can catch, or hook, and begin turning before you are prepared to turn.

After you bevel the base edge of your ski, you need to bevel the side edge to maintain at least a 90-degree angle to the base edge (see figure 2.7). A 90-degree edge angle ensures a good grip or hold in the snow in a turn. You can put a more acute (less than 90-degree) angle in the edge to hold better on hard snow.

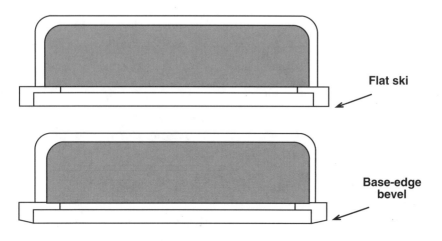

Figure 2.6 Base-edge beveling.

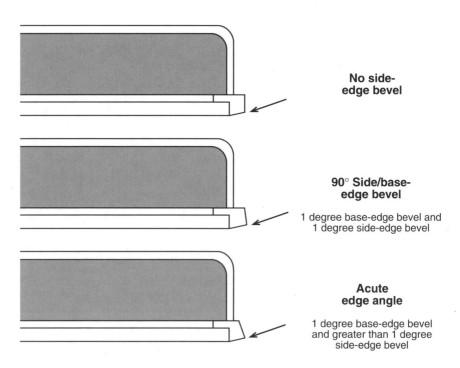

Figure 2.7 Side-edge beveling.

Be careful about falling into the trap of, "If a little is good, then a lot must be great." For base and edge beveling, start with a conservative angle and then experiment with different angles until you find the right one for your type of ski, your skiing style, and normal snow conditions:

- For soft snow (powder, moguls, Western-type snow): base-edge bevel—1 degree; side-edge bevel—1 degree
- For harder snow (recreational racing, artificial snow): base-edge bevel—1 degree; side-edge bevel—1.5 degrees

If your skis hook, or catch edges, increase the base-edge bevel in the tip and the tail. Increase the base-edge bevel by a degree over the first two to four inches of edge in snow contact. If the skis still hook, lengthen the increased bevel two inches at a time. Shaped skis may require this more than conventional sidecut skis.

Keep both edges of each ski sharp and beveled. The skis will perform better and you will not have drag from a dull edge or an edge with burrs. Also, by having each edge sharpened, you are better prepared for the unexpected. If you hit a rock and damage an edge, you can immediately switch skis and still have good, sharp inside edges for the rest of the day.

SKI WAXING

Wax your bases at least every third time you go skiing (ideally, every time) to keep your skis in top gliding form. When waxing, remember that (1) snow friction depends on snow and air temperature—changes in temperature create either wet friction from water or dry friction from snow crystals; (2) snow granulation is usually cataloged as new, old, or man-made snow—changes in snow type relate to crystal size; and (3) humidity affects the amount of moisture in the snow and causes wet friction.

It is important to wax.

1. Using the correct wax helps your skis respond to changes in snow conditions, enhancing their performance potential. Wax counters the suctioning effect of wet snow friction on the porous bases of your skis. Round snow crystals (old snow and slush) and warm temperatures demand softer wax than sharp

crystals (light, new-fallen snow) and cold air, which require hard wax.

2. You need less energy to push your skis when they are properly waxed.

3. Waxing protects your bases from excessive wear and from drying out.

Waxing would be complicated except that wax companies have made it simple for the skier. They have produced waxes for each set of conditions, and waxes that work in a wide range of conditions. They have made charts that outline when to use which wax. A set of one brand of waxes usually consists of two or three different waxes and the chart. If you follow the chart you will find that waxing becomes a simple and quick process.

Based on the weather, temperature, and snow conditions, select a wax or mix of waxes from the waxing chart. Heat a waxing iron or an old household iron to a midrange temperature. Melt the wax on the iron and allow it to drip on the ski. If the wax smokes, the iron is too hot (excess heat can damage the chemical properties of wax). Iron the wax into the ski being careful not to overheat the ski. A good rule of thumb is to have the iron hot enough so that as you move the iron forward, a wet pool of wax 6 inches to 10 inches long remains behind the iron. After the ski has cooled, scrape off all wax with a plastic scraper. Use the groove cleaner to remove wax from the base groove (many modern skis do not have a groove). Brush the base with a nylon brush to remove any additional wax. Your skis are now ready for high-performance skiing!

KEYS TO HIGH PERFORMANCE

1. Use modern clothing designed for skiing to provide comfort and function in high-performance skiing. Consider the types of skiing and climate.

2. Invest time selecting properly fitting boots. Boots are the most important piece of ski equipment.

3. Ensure high-performance skiing by modifying and adjusting your boots at a specialty ski shop.

4. For your skiing safety, make sure that your bindings are of modern design, properly adjusted, and in good working condition.

5. Know the design features of a ski and how they apply to skiing mechanics to better use your skis in high-performance skiing.

6. Skis are designed for specific types of skiing. When selecting skis for your type of high performance, consider the design features, talk to experts, and use demo skis before making a final selection.

7. Properly maintain high-performance skis so that they perform to their potential.

8. Learn the proper tuning techniques and acquire the appropriate tuning tools to maintain your own equipment. Specialty ski shops can also provide ski maintenance service.

9. Keep ski bases repaired and waxed for the existing conditions.

10. Keep ski edges sharp and maintain the appropriate edge angles.

CHAPTER 3

CONDITIONING FOR HIGH PERFORMANCE

If you want to be a high-performance skier you have to be tough with yourself, whether in the preseason off the snow, during the season, or at the beginning of your skiing day. High-performance skiing is skiing efficiently from the run's beginning to its end.

In the days of leather boots and relatively inflexible wooden skis, it took muscle to move the skis to create turns. Ski design and technique required more strength to turn the skis. Most turns looked acrobatic. With equipment and technique changes, strength is less important than your overall fitness for skiing at high-performance levels, while keeping the risk of injury low.

Getting in shape for skiing is a constant process of varied activities and personal achievement, based not on what you must do, but on what you choose to do. Break the year-round program into five seasons:

- During the **off-season**, focus on strength training and conditioning activities. Many sports and recreational activities can provide you with pleasurable fitness, mental intensity, skills application, and overall agility. Use the summer for triathlons, water sports, in-line skating, tennis, running, hiking, and early morning and late night gym workouts.

- The **preseason** is the four to six weeks before skiing begins. Concentrate on increasing key body area flexibility and overall body endurance. Decrease off-season strength training.

- The **early season** is the first two weeks of the season. Reacquaint your body to the movements of skiing. Focus on increasing flexibility and endurance (with weights), and speed or quickness (with conditioning).

- In the **skiing season**, when skiing is your sport and the other stuff just feeds it, remember that you need to maintain flexibility, strength and endurance (with weights), and conditioning activities that complement your level and amount of skiing.

- In the **postseason**, those several weeks in which you graduate to new sports interests or stay active for summer racing camp, focus on weight training and an appropriate shift in flexibility and conditioning strategies.

Be sure to maintain overall, year-round conditioning and flexibility. Whatever you lose by inactivity you must regain by diligent work. You are your own coach. You make the choices and, at times, the sacrifices to become stronger and fit.

PHYSICAL CONDITIONING

Physical conditioning is important because most recreational skiers do not ski enough days to ski themselves into shape. Because you exert a tremendous amount of muscular energy while skiing, improving your cardiovascular fitness allows you to get more oxygen to your muscles while exerting less effort. The more you ski, the more vulnerable you are to fatigue from exertion as well as from weather and snow conditions; fatigue leads to injury. If you are in good shape you can ski for a longer time without resting so that you can acquire high-performance skills more quickly.

Improve your fitness by exercising aerobically three to five times a week. Aerobic exercise includes running, particularly up and down hills to work the calves and quads and on uneven, curvy terrain to maximize use of ski-specific muscles; aerobics classes; swimming; serious cycling with loose arms to help work your gluteal muscles;

cross-country skiing; endurance in-line or ice skating; intense racquetball or squash; aggressive singles tennis; brisk walking or hiking, especially with a weighted pack; or any activity that increases your heart rate to 70 to 85 percent of your maximum heart rate (MHR) for at least 20 minutes. (Your MHR is 220 minus your age.) When your chosen activity becomes easy, intensify the aerobic workout by performing it for a longer duration or at a faster pace; this keeps it interesting and gives you the greatest benefit.

Make your exercises a reflection of your skiing; if you like to gun it while skiing, try the same in your off-season activities. Tailor activities to skiing style; if you like bumps, choose activities that make you work your legs in retracted and extended positions; if you are a racer, use activities that condition your legs for lateral and vertical quickness. Overall, exercise as ski-specifically as you can. Think of the muscles that are at work as both encouraging and resisting the forces inherent in skiing: hips, feet, fronts and backs of legs, abdominals, lower back, and buttocks, and work these both statically (isometrically) and dynamically (actively) to simulate how they are used in skiing.

Apply the concept of muscle specificity to your ski conditioning and training. Muscle specificity means that muscles are conditioned to respond to the demands they are given during habitual training. Be patient with your training, and give your muscle-tendon-joint complexes time to learn the coordinated movements required in high-performance skiing.

MUSCULAR STRENGTH

Muscular strength is essential for dynamic skiing. Skiing involves diverging steps, skating, explosive reactions to terrain changes, and defensive pole-plants in the steeps and in unexpected mogul situations. All of these activities require leg and upper body strength. Dynamic skiing also involves keeping your center of mass moving squarely down the fall line, which requires abdominal and pelvic-region strength. Racing and turning involve steady and sturdy downhill legs. Racers need a strong upper body for their powerful start. And finally, adaptation and recovery from errant attempts to take it to the edge require overall body strength.

Guidelines for Building Strength

- Approach strength building slowly and meticulously. When lifting, exhale on the lift and inhale during the rest. If it takes two to three seconds to lift, use four to six seconds to bring the weight back to the starting position. Generally, do 8 to 10 repetitions of each lift per set; do two to three sets per weight exercise or routine; and do a resistance workout on one set of muscles two or three days a week.

- When the lifting feels too easy, increase the weight. During the first month of a serious strength-building routine you should increase weekly the amount of weight you're lifting. Rest 60 to 90 seconds between each exercise in a set to re-oxygenate your muscles.

- Allow a day between workouts of a particular muscle system to allow for repair. The one exception is when you first get started. Repeat the same lifts for four to five consecutive days to acquaint your body with the new exercises and to get rid of the muscle pain you'll experience due to neural aches and lactic acid. To achieve a baseline level of strength for recreational skiers, we recommend a basic, total-body weight workout every other day, three days a week, with or without the use of free weights.

- Try to include dynamic expressions of strength in your program to give you the incentive to keep working or to modify workouts to accomplish your goals. These can be dramatic lifts of weights, extreme exertion sports, or leaping-bounding against resistance, for instance. Remember your goal: to build dynamic strength that provides power and durability when you are in motion or responding to stimuli on the slopes.

- Build strength in balance—a lack of balanced strength in opposing muscles contributes to injury.

- Consult an athletic trainer, a weight coach, qualified weight room staff, or weight-training books for guidance for your lifting needs.

INCREASING MUSCULAR STRENGTH

Develop muscular strength by doing plenty of isotonic strengthening exercises for your legs and upper body—that is, exercises where you move your legs and upper body against increasingly heavy resistance (there should be an exertion/lifting phase and a relaxation phase for these exercises). While a foundation of general upper and lower body strength is desirable, a program of daily abdominal, lower back, and pelvic strengthening is essential.

There are eight ski-specific areas to build into your training.

Abdominals

The very best combination exercise is the "protective sit-up" where you lift only your shoulder blades off the floor and make small contractions of your abdominal muscles. Do small lifts, straight ahead, with your hands behind your head (see figure 3.1) or out-stretched. You can also place your hands behind your head, elbows to the sides, touching one elbow to the opposite knee. To use your pelvis and lower back in the exercise, vary the positioning of your feet while keeping them off the floor: fan them out as in the splits, hold them off the floor with your knees bent and lower legs parallel to the floor, or hold them and your legs perpendicular to the floor (see figure 3.2).

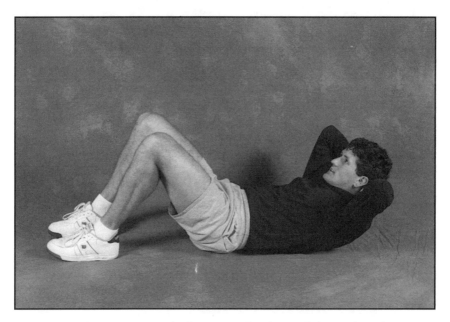

Figure 3.1 Basic protective body position for doing abdominal work.

Figure 3.2 Press your lower back against the floor and your chin to your chest as you repeatedly, but slowly, reach your hands forward two to three inches with each lift.

You should begin with repetitions in the 10s and go as high as several hundred to a thousand or more repetitions of mixed abdominal strengthening exercises. For example, you could repeatedly, but slowly, lift your shoulder blades off the floor and reach your hands through your knees. Or, you could focus on pressing your lower back against the floor and your chin to your chest as you repeatedly, but slowly, reach your hands forward two to three inches with each lift. You could also start with your back on the floor, and alternately touch one elbow to the opposite knee, returning to the floor between each contraction.

Quadriceps and Hamstrings

To build dynamic strength in your quads (thighs) you need to exercise them against resistance while moving (or against resistance right after activity). Do this by hill running, stairclimbing, hiking, step aerobics, and sprinting. With weights, do half-squats, quad extensions, and incline leg presses where your back is protected. Follow the weight work with running (outdoors, indoors, or on the treadmill), walking, aerobics, cycling, or easy-pace stairclimbing. All weight-resistant quad work should be complemented by weight-resistant work on the hamstrings (backs of the thighs).

Hip Extensors and Flexors

There are weight resistance machines for hip extensors and flexors. The physiology staff at your local health club can help you. Half-squats and incline leg presses are beneficial, as are step aerobics, outdoor stairclimbing, hiking, and boulder-bounding.

Calves and Ankles

In addition to the dynamic exercises noted above, toe raises with weight resistance are ideal for strengthening the calves and ankles. There are machines and apparatus designed to provide calf and ankle development with resistance. Hopping with added mild weight resistance is beneficial if the athlete's calves and ankles are already strong. Also, plyometrics (i.e., dynamic bounding in a controlled space to achieve specific movements) is highly productive to the fit athlete.

Lower Back

Along with the abdominal exercises noted earlier, an excellent lower back strengthener is the cable pull-down, where resistance is used while kneeling and doing abdominal curls. To modify the pull-down to develop the lower back, do the exercise with a flat back all the way through, rather than curling at the waist toward the end of the pull-down. There are resistance machines especially for the lower back.

Chest

The classic chest-builder, the bench press, remains the exercise of choice. Standard, incline, and decline bench presses are all useful, depending on your comfort and familiarity with these exercises. The standard bench press can be done with a free bar or fixed machine lift. There is also other equipment to exercise and develop chest strength. For the more adventuresome, there are "medicine ball workouts" (where a weighted ball the size of a basketball is tossed person to person, midsection to midsection), exercise cords, an assortment of push-ups, and myriad dumbbell adaptations that can be used to develop chest strength.

Upper Back

There are resistance machines specifically for the upper back, and for many people, these are the best and safest option. There are also dumbbell exercises that strengthen the shoulders, providing complementary strengthening to the upper back. A highly beneficial dumbbell exercise for the shoulders is done standing. Facing a mirror, hold lightweight dumbbells with arms to your sides. Keeping your arms straight, slowly raise them to shoulder level, forming a "T"; hold for a two-count and then slowly lower. Repeat 6-8 times; rest for 60 seconds and repeat this sequence two more times. A dumbbell exercise for the upper back is done with an incline bench. Facing the bench, lean your chest against the length of the incline. Holding lightweight dumbbells in a bear hug fashion around the back of the incline bench, slowly pull your elbows and arms back, arms bent, to effect a pinching together of your upper back, at all times keeping your upper body against the bench. As above, hold for a two-count and repeat.

Shoulders and Upper Arms

Free weights offer athletes a broad range of strength-building options for the shoulders and upper arms. These exercises provide some of the most fun for the recreational lifter, with some of the most pronounced effects for the effort. There are two classic free weight exercises for the shoulders and upper arms. The traditional military press, where the bar is first lifted to shoulder level and then repeatedly lifted overhead, can be done with varying poundages and repetitions depending on your level of muscular development. The other classic free bar exercise is the biceps curl, where hands are cupped under the free bar at hips' width, and the bar is curled up to chest level with elbows "pasted" to your hips. Again, use varying poundages and repetitions.

FLEXIBILITY

Stretching, as a complement to strength workouts, will improve your agility and quickness. When you strengthen your muscles, you also shorten them. Stretching lengthens the muscles again, leading to flexibility that allows you to move effortlessly without strain.

Flexibility enables you to get the most out of your strength and conditioning program and allows you to ski aggressively, in control, and in a relaxed, fluid state using a minimum of energy. Flexibility also provides muscle elongation when you have to react, adapt, and contort to awkward positions in order to right yourself during an impending fall or out-of-balance move—especially common on race courses and in the bumps.

Flexible skiers ski longer and harder with less fatigue because they use their increased range of motion in muscle-tendon-joint complexes to decrease the amount of muscular contraction needed to keep them in balance while skiing.

INCREASING FLEXIBILITY

Stretch only after your body is warmed up; fill the muscles with blood before stretching. Once you are warmed up, be patient while stretching: press into your stretches gently (never bounce), gradually increasing the length and duration of the stretch with each repetition.

We encourage people to stretch statically, that is, to press into a stretch, and hold for a count of 10 to 20 to the point at which the stretch begins to cause a mild tingling (not pain). Then either relax the stretch for another repetition, or press further and hold, continuing for as long as comfortable, each time reaching the point of mild tingling (the point at which you make gains in flexibility). If stretching is painful, you are probably tearing more than stretching the muscles.

Stretching can be fun. Play with a variety of stretches and opportunities for stretching. For some, the most convenient overall body stretch is provided by attendance at an aerobics class (preferably low-impact or soft aerobics) at least three days a week.

The every-day, post-exercise, at-home stretching leads to consistent, though incremental, increases in flexibility. Stretch to increase flexibility in parts of your body that you do not use every day, but that are essential to high-performance skiing. Include stretches for improving the lateral movement of your knees and ankles (see figure 3.3, a and b), the rotational movement of your femur (large bone of your thigh) in your hip socket, the movement of your trunk and arms (upper body) in the opposite direction from your knees and ankles (lower body), and the uncoiling movement of switching the upper and lower bodies to opposite sides.

Perform your stretches regularly, in an organized fashion, and in the proper environment. The worst programs are those that you feel forced to complete. We suggest the following stretches for six critical areas of a skier's body.

a

b

Figure 3.3, a and b The "C" stretch is great for the hips and ankles. Stretching from (a) to (b) is demanding, and the feet separate more to accomplish a good stretch. Must be held for a 10–count.

Trunk

To stretch the external oblique muscles on the sides of your waist and rib cage, use twisting stretches and side bends that stretch one side of your trunk at a time (see figure 3.4). Perform these stretches either statically or with very tiny stretches beyond the already stretched position.

Back

To increase flexibility in the lower back use stretches that encourage gentle elongation of the spine (see figures 3.5 and 3.6). Work the back and abdominals together. Do not perform stretches that strain the back, like bending at the waist while standing with knees locked. For

Figure 3.4 With your spine upright and one arm resting in your lap, reach across your body with the other arm, twisting your entire upper body to one side.

Figure 3.5 Kneel on all fours in a flat–back position while looking at the floor. Contract your abdominal muscles and tilt your pelvis under so that your back rounds up and forms an arch.

Figure 3.6 Lie face down on the floor. Place your palms flat on the floor near your hips. Press down on the floor and raise your torso as far as you feel is comfortable. Hold the stretch and repeat at least three times.

example, kneel on all fours in a flat back position while looking at the floor. Contract your abdominal muscles and tilt your pelvis under so that your back rounds up and forms an arch. Another helpful stretch is to lie face down on the floor, placing your hands flat on the floor near your hips. Press down on the floor and raise your torso as high as is comfortable. With both stretches, hold for a 6-10 count and repeat at least three times.

Knees

There are at least three exercises for increasing lateral flexibility in the knees. (1) Ski pole taps: squat with knees together and poles held in skiing position (perpendicular to the ground) outside your knees. Swing your knees side to side to touch your poles. (2) Stand erect and

Figure 3.7 Press the knees laterally to effect a stretching; hold for a 10-count and rise. Perform the stretch in the other direction.

counter-rotate your upper and lower body back and forth rhythmically, extending and flexing. (3) Jump in and out of a wedge (toes pointed in, heels out). The "in" movement is placing your feet together, parallel to each other, with your legs straight; the "out" jump is a large wedge with your legs slightly bent at the knees and ankles. This is a continuous-movement stretch.

Another exercise for knee flexibility is a stretch for the outside and inside of your knee. Stand with your side to a wall with your legs together, a couple of feet away. Lift your inside leg and allow your shoulder to fall gently into the wall. You will naturally angle or incline your outside leg toward the wall, creating a continuous stretch of the inside and outside of your knee. Switch sides.

A good standing knee flexibility stretch is done by standing tall and, while keeping your upper body "quiet," performing what amounts to lateral quarter-squats. Each time you bend your knees laterally to effect the stretch, hold for a 10-count and then rise to your starting position (see figure 3.7). Repeat to the other side. Begin with three and do as many as ten repetitions to each side. Do up to three sets.

Hamstrings and Groin

These muscles lie in the backs and insides of your thighs and run up into your crotch. To stretch these muscles, (1) sit on the floor and position your upper body over your outstretched thigh, (2) sit on the floor, open your legs wide, and work your upper body forward between your legs while maintaining a flat, straight back, (3) stand with your side to a counter and raise one leg onto the counter with the inside of your foot flush against the counter top; reach down and touch the outside of the ankle of the foot on the ground for a 5 to 10 count. Your legs should form a square with the floor and side of the counter.

An important two-part stretch for the hamstrings, Achilles, calves, and groin is performed by first placing your legs in a short-stride position on the floor, feet flat. Lean your upper torso forward, trying to keep a level back (see figure 3.8a). Hold the stretch for a 10-15 count. The second phase of the stretch is to place your legs further apart, feet flat, and lean your upper torso onto your thigh, head facing forward for the best stretch (see figure 3.8b). Again, hold for a 10-15 count and repeat the two-step sequence two or three times.

Figure 3.8, a and b A stretch for the hamstrings, Achilles, calves, and groin.

Hips

Focus on the rotational socket where the femur joins the pelvic bone. Lie on your back with arms outstretched. Cross one leg over the other in a scissors-like action, holding each scissors stretch for 10 to 20 seconds. Also, get down on all fours, lifting your leg laterally to isolate the action in the hip joint (see figure 3.9).

Quadriceps

Your quads perform a lot of the stability and endurance work while skiing. Stretch them with these exercises: (1) Stand erect and bend one leg at a time, grabbing the foot of the bent leg behind your back and pulling it to stretch the front of your thighs and your knees (see figure 3.10). (2) Squat down, "sitting" on the biomechanical platform created by this exquisite stretch (see figure 3.11). (3) Lie on your left side with your left arm supporting your head. Bend your right leg

Figure 3.9 Lift your leg with your knee bent to work the hip joint and abductor and adductor muscles. Work one side at a time.

Figure 3.10 Slowly pull the leg back until you feel a good stretch in your upper thigh.

Figure 3.11 Squat down, "sitting" on the biomechanical platform created by this exquisite stretch.

Figure 3.12 Lunge stretch with emphasis on stretching your front quadriceps and rear Achilles and calf. Done to each side.

and grab your right ankle. Slowly pull the leg back until you feel the stretch in your upper thigh. (4) Do lunge-type stretches in which you place one foot on its toes well behind you and the other foot in front of you and flat on the ground directly beneath its knee (see figure 3.12).

CONDITIONING COOL-DOWN AND REST

Each moderate or heavy workout session should include a cool-down to lower your heart rate gradually to near-resting level, and to get excess blood out of your extremities. Without a cool-down, excess extremity blood may cause sluggish circulation, lightheadedness, and post-activity soreness.

You can cool down effectively by keeping moving while reducing the demand on your heart to pump oxygenated blood: walk, jog slowly (following a brisk run), stair-step slowly, cycle slowly, swim easily with a pull buoy, or repeat the main exercise activity in a greatly toned-down manner.

A critical part of your conditioning program is planned rest. Rest is important for rejuvenating your mind, relaxing your muscles, and preventing overuse injuries. There are several ways to rest. The most obvious is sleeping, but other ways include meditation or reflecting on fond memories, painting, drawing, craftswork, and singing, as well as taking a hot bath, sitting in a hot tub or sauna, and receiving a full-body massage.

Rest pauses, although different than the planned rest days in your conditioning program, help prevent injuries while skiing fatigued (the time when most injuries occur). If you are feeling tired and unresponsive on your skis, pause to rest (at the side of the run and in plain sight) several times during your last run. If your fatigue is intermittent, pause to rest between runs, do relaxation exercises while riding the chairlift, shake out your arms and legs, and even stop to do some on-snow stretches. Skiing fatigued should be the exception on any ski day.

WARMING UP FOR HIGH-PERFORMANCE SKIING

Athletes in any sport who want to prevent injuries and enhance athletic performance use an individually designed warm-up progression. Warm-ups increase your heart rate without stressing or stretching your muscles and tendons before the blood (oxygen- and nutrient-rich) has filled your muscles. The process of engorging your muscles is gradual, requiring at least 5 to 10 minutes. There are safe shortcuts used by highly trained and conditioned athletes who achieve sufficient engorgement and high ranges of flexibility sooner because of their greater cardiac output. Even these athletes, however, *gradually* work the torso and limbs.

The high-performance skier warms up to (a) decrease the risk of injury; (b) keep the body flexible and ready to adapt to changes in snow conditions, terrain, or other demands on the body; and (c) be able to ski with the highest level of efficiency. Most racers and competitive skiers admit that they ski better after a high-energy warm-up.

Warm muscles stretch more than cold muscles. A warmed-up, flexible body can absorb the shock of falls, off-balance compressions, and awkward positions better than a body that is not warmed up.

We tend to lose flexibility as we age, beginning in the late twenties. Young people can function on the slopes with little or no warm-up. They play more with the snow and ski less intensively and less aggressively. For skiers over age 30, daily stretching is crucial both before and after skiing. Use a series of warm-ups each time you go skiing to help maintain your flexibility and versatility throughout the ski season:

1. Do early morning sit-ups to warm the body. Strong and toned abdominal muscles are one of the greatest allies to centered skiing and a problem-free back.

2. Fill your muscles with blood by exercising to make your heart beat faster and your large muscles work harder, but not excessively, for 5 to 10 minutes. Then begin stretching (a) the fronts and backs of the legs, (b) the inner thighs and groin, (c) the lower back, (d) the mid-section, and (e) the shoulders and neck. In the process of stretching the inner thigh, groin, and legs, you will also exert proper stretch to the knees and ankles. Table 3.1 shows some on-snow activities you can use to begin or enhance your warm-up.

3. Use your first chairlift ride to stretch. Work your shoulders by rolling them forward (imagine making small circles at your shoulder joints), then reverse direction and roll them back. Repeat this sequence 3 times with 5 to 10 repetitions each. Second, work the back neck muscles by leaning your head to the right over your right shoulder, then slowly roll your head forward in a semicircle until your chin is nearly resting on your chest. Continue rolling slowly until your head is over your left shoulder. Then roll your head back in the other direction, over your chest to your right shoulder. Repeat twice. Third, rework your shoulders by pressing them down into your upper arms and holding for five counts. Lift them up toward your ears, holding for five counts. Repeat three times.

If you have room, twist your lower body (legs together) to the left, while you twist your upper body (at the mid-section) to the right (see figure 3.13). Hold for 7 to 10 counts and switch sides: lower body right, upper body left. Repeat as many times as you can, working on your upper and lower body separation—twist to the extremes and hold a tight separation during the 7-to-10 count. You might try bringing your inside ski up slightly during the exercise to achieve even greater separation. Be careful not to catch your skis on the lift towers.

Work your thighs and knees by lifting your lower legs slowly, your legs out straight, skis perpendicular to the snow. Lift one leg at a time or both legs together. Hold for at least 10 to 20 seconds each time (see figure 3.14). For safety reasons and effect, do the leg-lift movements slowly and avoid rocking the chair.

4. After you have warmed up, use your first run or two for acquaintance drills, and follow these with more stretching. All you want to do with these runs is loosen up and integrate your flexibility stretches with your skiing body. Start your first run very relaxed, building to more aggressive skiing by the run's end. Try basic wedge turns for a hundred yards; stem (skidded) wedge turns for 50 yards;

Figure 3.13 While seated on the chairlift, turn the upper body one way and the skis and lower body the other way. Hold the stretch for 10–20 seconds and repeat to the other side. Switch back and forth 3–5 times.

Figure 3.14 The skier contracts the quads and lifts one ski up perpendicular to the snow. Done slowly to both sides for a 10–20 count, this is an excellent chairlift exercise. After several single leg lifts, the skier can raise both skis to become perpendicular to the snow. This shouldn't have any bouncing or swinging movements to it.

converging step turns without skidding; and matched ski turns without skidding. On your second run, add a series of diverging turns with some attempts to ski on a single ski, turning it in both directions; then "ski loose."

Two stretches to perform with skis on are (a) lean down and touch, or lean as far as you can toward, the tips of your skis (see figure 3.15), and (b) stand tall, both poles steadying you; lift one ski and place its tail in the snow so it is tall in front of you; slowly lean into the raised knee to stretch the back of your leg (see figure 3.16).

Figure 3.15 Begin to lean forward; gradually increase the stretch in your legs and upper body to touch the tips of your skis.

Figure 3.16 Stretch your hamstrings with a 10-20 count, leaning as far forward as you can. Use your poles for balance.

5. Use your warm-up time to think about how you want to ski on this particular day (aggressively, casually, fast, quick, stylishly, efficiently), knowing that when you complete your stretching you will be ready to ski at your level of high performance.

6. You are ready to take a "glory run." Ski the way your body feels like skiing and let your mind take a vacation. This run can set the stage for the rest of the day.

Table 3.1

Any of the following, done for 5 to 10 minutes,
prepares your body for preliminary stretches.

Activity	Where	High Fitness Level	Low Fitness Level
Sidestep	A flat area	Slowly to moderately	Slowly
Herringbone walk	An easy slope	Moderately to a short four- to eight-step sprint	Very slowly
Sidestep	An easy slope: step up and down	Moderately	Slowly
Ski skate	Flat open space	Moderately to quickly	Slowly to moderately
Ski skate	Down uncrowded bunny slopes or comfortable terrain	Moderately to quickly	Slowly to moderately
Baby rounders (make as many little turns as you can down the run)	Gentle slope	Slowly to moderately	Slowly to moderately

KEYS TO HIGH PERFORMANCE

1. A high-performance skier must be technically sound, physically fit, aggressive when exercising, committed to off-season and in-season training, and psychologically sharp.

2. Train in all seasons: off-season, preseason, early season, ski season, and postseason.

3. Most recreational skiers do not ski frequently enough to ski themselves into shape. For these skiers, aerobic exercise and conditioning are essential.

4. Dynamic skiing requires dynamic as well as static muscular strength to skate, take step turns, react to dramatic terrain

Foods and Fluids On and Off the Slope

Food is energy. You must eat—and eat properly—to be active. We consider the following to be the quintessential elements of ski nutrition.

1. All the oxygen in the world will not provide your body with the blood glucose it needs to fire its muscles. Carbohydrates are the foods used most readily to fuel the alpine skier. In the absence of carbohydrates for the start–stop energy used for high-performance skiing, the body uses fat, and finally breaks down protein.

Average recreational athletes need at least 1,000 to 1,500 pure *energy calories* beyond their basic metabolic requirement (BMR) for each day of activity (on rest days caloric needs may vary). Complex and simple carbohydrates should comprise all of these energy calories and 80 to 90 percent of the total calorie intake for the day. Here is a look at the proportions of major nutrients you need: 80 percent carbohydrates (about 65 percent complex and 15 percent simple); 12 percent lean protein; 5 to 8 percent fats (butter, whole milk products, meat fat, poultry skin, oils, fried foods).

2. Alpine skiing is not an endurance sport; therefore fatty foods play only a complementary role in your "ski nutrition" performance diet.

3. Breakfast is the most important meal for a day of skiing. Snacks (including candy bars, fruit, trail mix, and assorted other goodies) and lunch complement a nutritious breakfast. It is highly productive to begin your ski day well fed with high-energy foods.

"Ski lunch" for most recreational skiers complements their breakfast. Your "ski lunch" depends on what you demand of your body in the afternoon. Skiing powder or mogul bashing until the lifts close requires a serious approach to lunch, both for your safety and your performance. You need to eat foods that provide energy to your exercising muscles, and you need to avoid foods that will diminish your energy and induce lethargy. Most skiers have had enough experience with food to know what perks them up and what causes lethargy.

4. Your body needs fluid before, during, and after strenuous skiing, whether or not you feel thirsty. It is possible to be close to dehydration and not feel thirsty.

Sweating is the body's mechanism for cooling itself. The more you sweat, the more fluid you lose and the more fluid you need to replace. Losing 3 percent of body fluid weight is considered safe, 5 percent is borderline, and 8 percent is dangerous. When you lose too much fluid without replacement, you are prone to dehydration. This is especially

→

noteworthy for spring skiing, but applies as well to full-day cold weather skiing.

There is one essential fluid: water! Water is the best source of fluid before and after athletic exertion. Other fluids we ingest may cause undesirable effects: caffeinated beverages are diuretic (fluid eliminating); sugar-based drinks can cause stomach cramps; and alcoholic beverages are diuretics and depressants that lower body temperature. You may drink soft drinks, tea, and coffee, but thinking of these as fluids for athletic performance is a bit misguided and perhaps risky.

It is best to drink in anticipation, just as you should eat in anticipation of energy demands. First, drink plenty of water before going skiing, regardless of whether it is hot or cold outside. Drinking small amounts of water at frequent intervals is a good idea, as is drinking cold water when you are in need of fluids (after sweating)—cold water is absorbed more quickly than warm water. If you do not live at a high elevation, pay special attention to your fluid intake at high altitudes—you will need to drink more water than usual.

At summer racing camp, cold water is usually available in jugs at the base of the chairlifts leading to the training courses. Have a drink of water every time you get on the lift.

changes, use an effective defensive pole-plant, and, in general, be resilient.

5. Flexibility stretches that complement strength workouts add versatility to your strength and power, making you more agile and quick.

6. Stretching should not be painful, but you need to feel some tension and tingling in the stretched muscle to improve flexibility.

7. Rest is important to rejuvenate your mind, relax your muscles, prevent injury, and give you time to dream.

8. Food is essential for energy; you must eat to be active.

9. Your body uses carbohydrates first, followed by fats and then protein. Protein is not a quick-energy food!

10. Eat with performance in mind: eat the right foods at the right times.

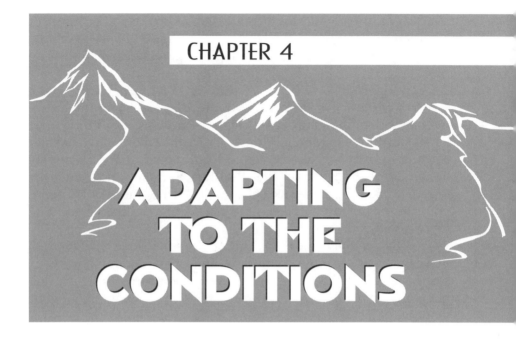

CHAPTER 4

ADAPTING TO THE CONDITIONS

Skiing offers a range of challenges that can vary from minute to minute, hour to hour, day to day, slope to slope, or mood to mood. Versatility is the spice of the sport. In this chapter we will discuss skiing several conditions: poor lighting, chopped-up powder, spring slush, machine-made snow "magels," mush, and hard, icy snow. These discussions will help you become more versatile and will sharpen your high-performance skiing skills.

APPROACHING THE FIRST DAY OF THE SEASON

Imagine that it is the first day of the season, the snow is just right, and you and your equipment are ready to go. First, do not expect to start off the season at the level of skiing you had achieved by the end of the previous season. Review the basics. Take an easy hill and go through a progression of skiing exercises to reacquaint your body with the feeling of skiing. Rediscover what it feels like to be on the snow; find the center of your skis. Relax; do not muscle your skis around.

Instead of tipping your skis on edge right away, do wedge turns for a half hour or so. There is a greater risk of injury if you ignore the reacquaintance period and cut to highly aggressive skiing the first day out.

Set pride aside, and begin with fairly static wedge turns, then slowly add the active steering of your turning ski. Next, add movement by extending your legs to begin your turns and flexing your knees and ankles to complete your turns. Add a more active transfer of your weight, foot to foot, leg to leg. Progress to an intentional lightening of one inside ski, then the other. Speed up and change the terrain until the lightened ski starts to match the other. At this point, you will begin to experience the inside or uphill ski becoming involved with steering.

To get a complete feel of the skis on the snow, let the skis skid to make the turns very round and slow, almost like manipulating your skis to drag out the turns. These are patient turns in which you gradually adjust to the conditions rather than rushing to suit your fantasies of last season.

Slowly reacquainting yourself with skiing the first day out gives you the opportunity to make subtle corrections in your skiing *now*. You can correct the way you approach wedge turns, extension and flexion, pole action, independent foot–leg action, and steering with your inside ski early in the season before last year's old habits reappear.

Using basic, slow exercises to sharpen these skills will automatically incorporate them into your skiing. Do not rush; take time to allow your natural movements to re-emerge. Use the first day to go through your basic skills and recall the higher performance skills that got you to where you left off last season.

POOR LIGHTING

You are in flat light when everything looks drab and it is hard to discern contours, angles, or ridges in the snow. This can be frightening, especially when the light changes suddenly. In poor lighting the visual stimuli are missing that help you adjust your balance to stay in control of your skiing. Your other senses need to pick up the slack. You need to be more sensitive to feel (with your feet, hands, and face, for example) and sound. First, however, slow down. One way to reduce your speed is to put more shape and roundness in your turns.

Stay centered over your skis, and stand tall so that you can make subtle adjustments to the terrain that you cannot see, which might include ruts, bumps, ridges, or concave and convex characteristics.

Skiing centered over your skis, standing tall, and relaxing make it easier to adapt your skiing to varying conditions. By standing tall you establish the sufficient *range of motion* needed to make subtle adjustments in your skiing. By skiing more slowly, you feel the direction and character of the slope. If you are skiing fast in poor lighting, you may tend to lean back into the hill, which will throw you off balance when you encounter abrupt terrain changes.

In addition to slowing down and staying tall, open your stance, which will improve your balance. Ski within range of trees or other non-snow landmarks that provide a focal point. Use the shadowed areas near trees, large rocks, trail signs, chairlifts, and other objects as visual aids to maintain balance—they will help you read how the terrain slopes or falls away. Also, look ahead, as this will establish a horizon and help your balance.

When skiing in poor lighting, let your skis tell you about the conditions via tactile sensations and sounds. Listen and feel to adapt and guide yourself in poorly lit conditions.

If you haven't done much skiing in poor lighting, try a pole-sensing exercise. Select a turn with which you feel comfortable, for example, a medium-radius turn. Open your stance and look for landmarks to establish your bearings. Lightly drag your poles and feel what they tell you about the snow, slope, and terrain. Dragging your poles will also help keep you centered. As the pitch of the hill changes, the feel of your poles changes accordingly; that is, if the hill slopes to the left, you'll feel your left pole dropping away from you. In this way, your poles serve as sensors as do your feet (see figure 4.1).

The more information you acquire about the skiing conditions, the more you can ski them in a high-performance mode.

SKIING CRUD (AND LIKING IT)

Crud is thick and heavy snow that is difficult to ski in the deeper sections. Imagine that two days ago a foot and a half of snow fell, and after getting cut up, it has settled over the mountain. On the groomed runs the snow is smooth and fast, but off the groom where the challenge calls, there are 8 to 10 inches of cut-up snow, with mounds up to a foot deep. Although the lighting is sufficient, and the snow

Figure 4.1 Keep your tips on the snow during this pole–sensing exercise.

itself has dried out a bit from the overnight cold, the overall conditions in this unpredictable crud are demanding.

Skiing crud offers an exciting challenge. To be a truly versatile and high-performance skier you must learn to ski crud. Crud skiing is one of the least predictable conditions; it can occur anytime during the season. To enjoy skiing crud and difficult snow, you must incorporate aggressiveness, a high degree of ski–snow sensitivity, a blocking pole-plant, active extension and retraction (pushing out and pulling in) of your legs, balance, and strong rotary and steering skills. Lacking all or any of these, crud may seem foreboding, but by approaching the condition with some preparation and basic techniques, you can learn to make crud an enjoyable part of your skiing. First, consider what *not* to do when skiing crud.

1. *Don't* ski crud on flat to moderate terrain—the lack of momentum will lead to a lack of turning power.

2. *Don't* ski crud until you are psychologically ready for it—a tentative attitude leads to a lack of aggressiveness.

3. *Don't* ski crud aggressively until you are confident making parallel turns or up-stem–type turns (i.e., skidded turns initiated by the brushing out of your outside or downhill ski) on groomed slopes.

4. *Don't* ski crud until you have developed a sense of pole use in your skiing.

5. *Don't* ski crud until you have confidence in moguls and steeper terrain.

6. *Don't* ski crud in closed areas.

Avoid long-radius turns. In a long-radius turn there is a long gliding phase that is accompanied by little steering. The risk in crud is getting tangled in others' tracks at the point in your long-radius turn where you are not steering. In medium-radius turns, you apply stronger rotary skills and steering and are more able to brush away the snow in these railroad tracks. Muscling your skis around with abrupt movements might trip you up. If the slope is steep, use the more aggressive, sometimes more abrupt, short-radius turn.

Be more compact on your skis in most crud conditions. In other words, become shorter (see figure 4.2). You can be stronger in this

Figure 4.2 Sometimes a more compact stance can give you more power in the crud.

(continued)

Figure 4.3, a-d Dynamic movements explode the snow away from your skis.

Figure 4.3, a-d *(continued)*

position and have better control (because of the shorter angles that are created) to deal with unexpected changes in the conditions and terrain. If you stand tall, you are vulnerable to being rocked backward or thrown off balance.

Game Plan for Beginning Crud Skiing

Use gravity. The steeper the terrain, the greater your momentum, and the easier it is to guide or steer your skis into each new turn. Knowing that you have gravity on your side makes it easier to maintain an aggressive "I can ski this" attitude.

1. Ski with a friend in case either of you needs help in the event of an untimely tumble.

2. Sample the crud by standing, walking, hopping, and pushing your skis around in it.

3. Summarize the run you intend to take, and identify suitable exits you can make if the crud is too unfriendly.

4. Start into the terrain with an aggressive attitude, carrying good speed into your early turns. If the conditions call for it, you can decrease your speed. If you start off slowly, it is not easy to accelerate.

5. Try a few medium-radius turns to a planned exit, and see how the crud feels. As a beginner, you may need or want to rotate your whole body to get your skis into each new turn. Do this relative to the turn dynamics discussed later, and continue to practice it until you develop the confidence to keep it up for an entire run. In time, you will slow the rotary movements of your upper body while actively extending and retracting your legs as you leap out of one turn and into another. (In heavy crud, 90 percent of your turn is done during the leaping phase in which your legs are retracted and your feet are steered or guided in the direction of your new turn.)

6. Use your pole plant as an additional sensor and to momentarily block your upper body from moving down the hill while your legs are pulled out of the snow, guided into the new turn, and extended back into the snow. The extension of your legs (see figure 4.3, a-d) and bending of your skis against the snow actually pushes the snow downhill, creating a platform against which you ride your skis and off of which your skis are deflected as you retract your legs and guide your skis into your new turn.

It's All About Your Mind-Set

It was one of those infamous days in the Lake Tahoe-area Sierras when the snow was wet, deep, and partially groomed by snowcats and skiers. Riding up the lift, a student asked me how the skiers below us seemed to just float through the wet snow, making skiing in this tricky condition look effortless.

Clearly, their skiing wasn't without effort. Certainly they had skill, but all the skill in the world won't make you versatile in a broad array of conditions without the right mental readiness. What these skiers had was the right mind-set. They had learned how to take the thought out of skiing and just go with the terrain, and they showed it by how they approached the conditions.

Taking the thought out of skiing and going with the terrain is a mind-set of nonjudgmentalness and ingrained cunning. It's a mind-set of viewing the conditions as neither bad nor good, but as moments or episodes of changing snow and terrain to which one must respond instinctively with automatic skill execution. Skiers with such a mind-set appear to float because they've taken the work out of skiing and stopped planning their next move or series of moves. They're just "happening" on the snow.

Of course, this state of "happening" isn't something that occurs overnight, nor is it something you can will to happen. It takes plenty of time out on the mountain thinking about your skiing, planning moves in different conditions, using the tips in this book, and often calculating certain descents.

A certain commitment to ski drills and exercises is still important, and while doing them you can excuse what might appear to be an overuse of your thoughts and judgments in skiing. Remember, when you're doing ski drills and exercises you're *supposed to think about your skiing*, and in the most judgmental of ways.

The ability to separate learning to ski better (i.e., exercises and drills) from free skiing (i.e., skiing just to ski and have fun) is key to developing a mind-set for versatile condition skiing. Although there is no set formula for the balance between drills and free skiing, it's generally safe to break up your ski season or ski time so that you do more drills in the early season and more free skiing later in the season. Similarly, if you go skiing only a few times a season, you might want to set aside the first hour of your day to do drills, and then free ski for a couple of hours before lunch. If you're feeling good after lunch, go out and drill for another 30 to 60 minutes and then free ski until the lifts close.

When you take a "drill first, free ski later" approach to your skiing, you find it easier to develop a skiing style that's natural for you. The reason really good skiers appear to float down the hill in every sort of condition is that they're skiing in a style that's natural and right for their bodies, their biomechanics, and their attitude about skiing. They learned long ago to get their thoughts about how to ski (or not ski) out of their heads, and to just ski relaxedly and confidently.

Given enough patience and time out on the hill, you may well find yourself starting to ski relaxedly and confidently, appearing to others as if you're floating down the slopes. But the first step to achieving this is getting out in all sorts of conditions and expanding your comfort zone.

Figure 4.4 Blast around in the crud.

7. Go into crud knowing that the crud will probably get the better of you, but that after repeated exposure you will have your day. Try not to be discouraged by unexpected tumbles.

8. Ski crud like a kangaroo, using the strength of your legs to bound in and out of the snow (see figure 4.4). If you can master difficult snow, your lightness and ski–snow sensitivity in powder and other snow conditions will excel.

Strategies for Heavy Crud

Simultaneous leg–foot rotation works well for non-aggressive skiers because they are moving the skis as a single force against stubborn snow. Aggressive skiers often use this approach in heavily chewed-up, deep crud. Along with simultaneous leg–foot rotation, ski heavy crud with a compact stance and with your skis on top of the snow. To accomplish the former, use retraction (i.e., bring your knees up toward your chest); to accomplish the latter, lighten the pressure of your skis on the snow by keeping your toes up off the snow.

Developing Versatility in Crud

Ski crud with an aggressive attitude. It is usually easier to "roll back" an aggressive attitude to suit less demanding conditions than it is to muster an aggressive attitude in difficult crud.

a

b

Figure 4.5, a and b Rely on independent leg action and retraction for versatility in the crud.

When skiing crud, use a combination of independent and simultaneous foot–leg action (see figure 4.5, a and b). Use independent foot–leg action to guide or steer your skis into your turns, then engage simultaneous action to ride your skis through the belly and finish of your turns. The independent foot–leg action is instrumental in achieving proficiency and aggressiveness in crud; the simultaneous foot–leg action helps to stabilize the completion of your turns.

If you want to learn to ski crud, request a ski school lesson, private or group, that is oriented to these conditions. If enough students request such a class, one will likely be scheduled.

SKIING SPRING SLUSH OR SOFT SNOW

Although soft, wet, sticky slush is not always attractive to hearty winter skiers, these conditions can help improve your rotary skills, edge pressure, fore and aft leverage, and balance, as well as providing an opportunity to try a variety of otherwise foreboding terrains.

Spring's warm days and cold nights produce *corn snow*—little ball-bearings or kernels of snow that develop from the overnight freezing and early morning thawing of surface snow. For high-performance skiers, *corn snow* offers wonderful opportunities and adventures, like unique skiing conditions in wide open terrain and the exploration of hidden, in-bound, tree-lined corridors that receive early morning sun at just the right time. Corn snow provides an opportunity to be mentally aggressive yet physically subtle, even artistic, in your skiing.

As the day goes on and more people ski the corn, the once-inviting snow changes to slush. The warmer the weather gets, the deeper and wetter the snow becomes. Problems arise when dirt, pine tar, exhaust from grooming machines, dust, oil, and other debris build up on the bases of your skis and cause drag and poor ski and skier performance.

To prevent these conditions from ruining your spring skiing, take care of your skis and consider the following techniques and strategies.

1. Keep the bases of your skis as clean as possible.
2. Avoid skiing across the fall line on any terrain where the slush is wet and deep—the added drag in the slush will quell your momentum, which you need in such snow.

3. Keep your skis light on the snow.

4. Do not complete your turns as you would in firmer snow conditions. Too complete a turn will lead to additional drag and a loss of momentum.

Use the Conditions

Once you get on steeper, more demanding terrain, you may want to use the slowing effect of spring snow to control your speed (see figure 4.6). It is also advantageous to use the natural resistance of the snow and the shape of the terrain to create turning adventures. The art of skiing spring snow involves taking advantage of its characteristics on terrain that you might not have skied during more firm-packed conditions. Some of the challenges include steep bump runs that encourage development of your pole plants, and areas in the trees alongside or in between marked runs. *Remember: closed areas are off limits!*

Use Your Tracks

Skiers can improve their skills when they take advantage of the many challenges of spring conditions. Corn snow, for example, offers an

Figure 4.6 Use wet snow to decrease your momentum and create stability in spring snow.

opportunity to review your skiing through an examination of your tracks. Try a series of medium- and short-radius turns. Critique your tracks in the corn. Are they symmetrical, rounded, S-shaped, Z-shaped? Next, look at your tracks to see how you make your turns. Are you skidding early in the turn or late? Are you riding predominantly one ski or two? Are you carving through the snow? Are you skiing a parallel or wedge-type turn?

Float Your Inside Ski

An effective strategy to try during your spring skiing is floating or lightening your inside ski. Do not put much weight on your inside or uphill ski while turning. You should actually lighten it early in your turn, and leave it lightened as you steer it through the turn. Let your inside ski ride along the top of the snow while the outside or downhill ski is working or being guided or steered through the turn (see figure 4.7). Even if your outside ski is slowed by the slush, your inside ski will not be bogged down if it is kept light on the snow. Also, by

Figure 4.7 Lighten the inside ski in slush to help control the level of drag on your skis.

keeping your inside ski light, it is ready to take over the responsibilities of the turning ski as soon as you transfer your weight from your outside ski to your inside ski. This helps to minimize the drag or friction that develops on the base of your skis.

Follow the Sun

In the morning there is soft snow where the sun has been baking the slope. Ski here first and as the day progresses, follow the sun around the mountain, skiing the snow just softened; avoid staying in any one place after the snow is too slushy. On a hot day, ski the first run once or twice. As soon as it softens, seek the shady areas that are just beginning to receive sun. The warmth of the day will have begun to soften the snow in these areas, and the direct sun will make the skiing great. Follow the sun to add two or three more hours of top spring skiing to your day.

Later in the afternoon, assuming you are well rested, you might want to revisit the slopes you skied earlier in the day. By then, the runs may have firmed up. If there is a large enough swing in daytime temperatures you may find a little of the early morning corn on the late afternoon slopes. This can be enjoyable skiing if the corn isn't too chopped up.

Ski Early and Stop Early

Another aspect of spring skiing that you must address is fatigue. Ski early and stop early. If you plan to ski aggressively over varied terrain, start early in the day (taking rest breaks and drinking plenty of fluids), ski through lunch, and then call it a day.

MACHINE-MADE SNOW

Machine-made snow provides skiable terrain at times of low snowfall and minimum coverage. The success of snowmaking and mountain management technology has been a bonus for early season skiers. When machine-made snow is first groomed out on the trails it is a delight to ski, yet skiing on a base that is largely artificial presents some special situations worth mentioning: granular mush, rigid magels (i.e., artificial moguls), and dense hardpack, which is skied as if it were ice.

Granular Mush

The texture of granular mush is like spring slush, although it is often drier. Because it is quite dense, it is often difficult to brush out of the way. Granular mush can form in cold weather from excessive skier traffic, while true slush forms only in warm weather. Granular mush forms most readily when snowmaking is frequent, and because there is little natural snowfall, the artificial base grows from several inches to one to two feet or more.

As with spring slush, ski granular mush in the fall line, regardless of speed, and rarely across the hill, particularly not at a slow speed. Ironically, some of the slopes that produce granular mush are beginner and low-intermediate slopes. The best advice is to avoid skiing granular mush if your style is to rely on traversing the hill to control your movement down the slope.

If you are an aggressive skier, you can ski granular mush dynamically in the fall line, ski to ski with long snake-like turns, floating the inside ski atop the granular snow while steering and variably pressuring the outside ski through the turn (see figure 4.8, a and b).

Variably pressuring the outside or turning ski is appropriate in all skiing, but in granular mush it is specifically safety-appropriate. As the texture and ski drag vary with respect to the depth and density of the mush, you must vary the amount of pressure applied to the turning ski. You can accomplish this by

a. using a forward flexing at the knee and in the lower leg to increase the pressure;

b. angling the knee or hip to increase the edge pressure on the ski;

c. retracting the leg in varying degrees to effect a reduction in pressure;

d. lifting your body off the snow to reduce pressure; and, for the very experienced,

e. transferring the pressure to the inside ski momentarily (or back and forth between skis without changing the direction of the turn).

Rigid Magels

The term *magel* distinguishes the different texture of moguls created from machine-made snow versus those developed from natural snow. Magels are a different breed of mogul, requiring hardpack- and ice-skiing skills.

Other distinctions of magels are purely circumstantial: they may be pointed and sharply cut, or they may be long and rounded like hard pancake moguls. In either case, magels may be rimmed by

Figure 4.8, a and b Lighten the inside ski when initiating a turn in loose snow.

mush. When this is the case, pay extra attention to your mogul-skiing style. Staying out of the trenches and skiing high on magels is a good idea.

Dense Hardpack

The texture of "skied-out" artificial snow varies according to its mix with natural snow, the air temperature, and its original crystalline development. Once the artificial snow, alone or mixed, has been repeatedly "heated" and compacted by ski bases gliding (and creating friction) over it, and by metal edges scraping it, the condition changes to hardpack. Hardpack may feel both slippery and sticky, "grabbing" your skis.

Treat this condition patiently. Ski it lightly in terms of edge pressure, but don't be afraid to ride your outside ski through the turn when the grip is stable. Dense hardpack is not skied as well with the on–off pressuring used successfully on ice, particularly if the hardpack is sticky.

HARD, ICY CONDITIONS

Should you go to the side of the run and start making short-radius turns? It would be a good way to check out the feel of the hill without diving into the icy conditions on the middle of the hill that result from skiers "kicking out" snow from the center to the sides. However, with very hard and icy snow this "kicked out" snow is not likely to be abundant.

The key to hard and icy conditions is to ski, rather than jam, the skis to an edge. It is a subtle, but critical, strategy for remaining relaxed and confident in these conditions. On ice, you often feel the sensation of sliding out of control. Many skiers' instinct is to hit the edges of their skis to stop the downhill sliding. Instead of slowing you down, however, this maneuver only creates even greater recklessness, during which your skis break loose, slide, and ensure that you remain out of control. This process will perpetuate itself until you do something to control your movement and speed.

To control your movement and speed, approach hard and icy conditions slowly. Approach the condition with slower, rounded, sliding turns, gradually guiding your skis (primarily the outside ski) onto an edge. As soon as you feel the ski's edge grab the snow ("bite"), move your weight off this turning ski and onto the other ski to begin the next sliding and gliding into an edge bite to make another turn (see figure 4.9, a-d). In icy conditions that offer little resistance to turning forces, anything more than quick on–off motions will create too much pressure. The consequence of too much pressure against little resistance is sliding out of control.

(continued)

Figure 4.9, a-d On ice, use just enough edge to get the skis to change direction.

c

d

Figure 4.9, a-d *(continued)*

Ski icy and hard conditions edge to edge, foot to foot, starting your turns with very light pressure on the turning edge of your ski. Gradually build up this pressure. Placing too much pressure on the edge will cause your skis to slide away from you. Liken it to Muhammed Ali's description of his fighting style: float like a butter-fly, sting like a bee. This is the essence of skiing ice: *sting* the ice to turn, *float* atop the ice to slide comfortably as you prepare to *sting* the snow again to initiate your next turn. If you continue steering and pressuring your skis with this *sting and float* approach, you'll be gradually tipping your skis onto their edges, carving on the hard snow.

KEYS TO HIGH PERFORMANCE

1. Make your first day of the season a high-performance day; go slowly, be patient, and review the basics. Rediscover what it feels like to be on the snow and centered on your skis. Do not be in a hurry to get your skis on edge, or to pick up this season's skiing where you left off last season.

2. When you cannot see changes in terrain, slow down, ski medium-radius turns, ski centered over your skis, and ski taller. Open your stance more than usual for a more stable base of support.

3. When skiing in poorly lit conditions, listen to what your skis tell you about the conditions via the sensations transmitted through your feet and sounds transmitted through your ears.

4. Lightly dragging your poles will help keep you centered. The poles act as sensors that detect changes in the snow, slope, and terrain.

5. Ski in crud with an aggressive attitude, though lightly on your skis. Ski with medium-radius turns because they are slow enough to check your speed yet fast enough to allow you to glide across the top of the crud. When you have finished one turn, move to your next turn immediately and smoothly. Muscling your skis around with abrupt movements is best reserved for steep, extraordinary crud.

6. Being aggressive means being emotionally and physically primed to respond quickly to changing conditions. Aggres-siveness is not measured by how hard or fast you ski.

7. Independent leg–foot action is instrumental for achieving proficiency in crud, although heavy crud may require a combination of independent and simultaneous leg–foot action.

8. In skiing slush, be light on the snow and do not complete your turns as fully as you might in firm snow conditions.

9. In skiing slush, float your inside ski so that it is lightly weighted and ready to be used for turning as soon as you shift your weight off the other ski.

10. In the spring, follow the sun around the mountain. Ski the snow that has just softened, but move on as the snow becomes slushy.

11. In the spring, ski early and stop early. If you ski all day, rest frequently and drink plenty of non-alcoholic fluids.

12. Machine-made snow presents opportunities to test your skills and apply specific skiing strategies to its challenging conditions.

CHAPTER 5

STEEP-SLOPE SKIING

The basic mechanics of skiing change little from condition to condition, although some steep-slope conditions require refinements to the application of basic skills. We have to decide how to apply our skills in the steeps relative to changes in terrain, snow texture, wind, temperature, pitch, other skiers, and how we are feeling at the time.

BARE ESSENTIALS
FOR SKIING THE STEEPS

There are at least two essentials for the steeps: good snow and a steady head.

Good Snow

In the steeps, good snow defines both safety and strategy. A steep chute that is packed with windblown snow is not nearly as appealing as a chute with newly fallen snow. Similarly, a steep chute that has "settled" a few days after a storm, and that has had little traffic on it because the top of the mountain was closed for avalanche control, is prime for skiing if you know the snow's texture and how to ski the chute. And then there is that most forgiving condition in a steep chute—corn snow or corn that has turned slushy.

Other steep-terrain snow conditions include slopes groomed by winch and snowcat, open moguls spread fairly wide apart (though most steeps offer just the opposite mogul configuration), and skier-packed bowls.

We do not recommend skiing steeps that have ice or hardpack snow, steeps with crunchy snow in its pre-corn frozen snow stage, and early groomed steeps that are replete with "death cookies" (hard chunks of ice and snow that groomers churned up overnight).

Steady Head

Skiers in the steeps need a steady head: a steady thought process and focus. A steady head is a matter of being confident in your ability, and dismissing any disruptive thoughts that could challenge you when you're skiing. Thoughts of doubt in the steeps lead to hesitancy and lack of flow, and jeopardize your performance and safety.

HIGH-PERFORMANCE SKILLS

In the steeps, extend your legs (knees, ankles, and hip joints) as an expression of the uncoiling of your countered upper and lower body, and push off your pole in a rebound-type manner to help direct your body mass into and down the fall line. Simultaneously, steer or guide your skis into the new turn, and flex your knees and ankles to hold an edge set platform that controls and completes your turn, leaving you ready for the next turn.

In the very beginning of the turn, be in a flexed and coiled position with your ankles and knees bent forward, and your skis together and edged in the snow. To uncoil, extend your legs and project your body down the fall line, which will feel like a free-fall down the mountain in the direction of your pole-plant. To effectively ski the steeps, you must learn to trust this extension outward and down the fall line with each turn (see figure 5.1, a-c).

Turns in the steeps have a dramatic preparation (the platform), a short initiation (during extension) where the skis are very light and follow the body around, a very brief control phase where the skis are steered with both feet (beginning flexion), and an abrupt finish (maximum flexion), which leads to new turn preparation.

Your uphill leg is short until you extend. As you extend and change direction (steer), your uphill leg becomes your downhill leg

a

b

(continued)

Figure 5.1, a-c A strong edge set, a solid pole–plant, and uncoiling ensures balance, speed control, and safety in the steeps.

c

Figure 5.1, a-c *(continued)*

and is very long and braced against the edged ski. Use the alternating lengthening of one leg and shortening of the other sequence when skiing the steeps, and avoid static skiing which leads to timidity, leaning back, locking your knees and hips, and using your poles little or not at all.

Here are some specific steep-slope skiing skills.

Solid Pole-Plant

The solid pole-plant that we rely on in the steeps is in sharp contrast to the pole-touch that we use as a timing device to add rhythm, as an additional terrain feeler, as a condition and balance sensor, and as a signal indicating the transfer of weight from the old turning ski to the new.

Imagine walking across a steep hill. As you traverse, half of your body is pulled downhill, while the other half shifts weight into the hill to keep you from falling. In the steeps it is critical to control the movement and momentum of your upper body as it follows gravity's lead downhill. The steeper the slope and angle of your descent, the stronger the pull of gravity, and the greater the need to control gravity's effect on your skiing.

In the steeps we use a blocking pole-plant to momentarily block the upper body from moving into the new turn before the legs have uncoiled. A solid pole-plant stabilizes your upper body at the critical time in a turn when you need to maintain control and balance, and helps keep your upper body facing down the fall line in a countered or anticipated position, allowing you to control all other movements necessary to safely and confidently ski the steeps.

In chapter 6 we will discuss the blocking action of a solid pole-plant in moguls.

Solid Pre-Turn

When you ski into a steep chute, look down the hill and seek the fall line, but do not attempt to pick up speed and then turn. Instead, make a pre-turn with a slight uphill steering of your skis in combination with your pole-plant to establish your first platform (see figures 5.2 and 5.3, a-c).

Figure 5.2 To control your speed in tight chutes, slightly turn your skis uphill before charging into steep terrain.

a

b   *(continued)*

Figure 5.3a-c Follow the lead of your first turn and continue to look down the hill.

c

Figure 5.3, a-c *(continued)*

Pre-turns are one of the more functional skills in the steeps, set up by a combination of good edge control and a solid pole-plant. One of the beneficial aspects of the pre-turn is psychological—once the pre-turn has been completed successfully you have momentarily established control of the steep terrain. If you can do it once, you can do it over and over again, skiing in control to the bottom.

Follow the lead of your first turn and continue to look down the hill and make turn after turn until you get to the bottom. This commitment to a series of three-point platforms (i.e., each ski set on edge and the tip of your pole planted downhill) will ensure consistent upper and lower body separation, helping you keep your upper body facing down the fall line. In this countered and anticipated position, your body is prepared to use its natural uncoiling to execute quick, smooth changes of direction once you release the pressure on your skis and pole.

Our Best Run in the Steeps

You never know when your best run will be; sometimes you don't know it even though you've just taken it. But when you think back to the hundreds of runs you've made, some stand out more than others.

No matter what your age, if you're like me, you ski for the thrill, and the thrill is fed as long as there are runs that challenge you to take it to the edge or to cut loose with friends or fellow skiers. Such runs are often steep, tree-lined runs found off the backside of your favorite resorts.

My best run, like a lot of others' out here in the Lake Tahoe area, started on Little Papoose, a beginners' slope at Squaw Valley. As might be expected, few skiers progress to the exhilaration of powder, when the "snow" melts off your lips and the powder's so deep you really can't see where you're going. As we progress to higher levels of skiing we try for runs nobody else has ever done—runs where we will be on the edge from the top to the bottom, runs where a fall means we won't stop until we get to the bottom, runs that stand out from all the rest: long, narrow, with deep powder, and the steepest we can find.

My friend Gary showed Elaine, Becky, and me where such a run was one day. After riding Chair Four at Kirkwood, we walked about two and a half hours in ski boots before we reached the top of Melissa Corey Peak in the Emigrant Lake Basin of the Sierra Nevadas, south of Lake Tahoe. We walked up that ridge line sweating, thirsty, tired, sore, and eager to reach our destination: the California Chute.

We stood at the top, still breathing hard, with sweat dripping from beneath our hats and looking down that steep chute. Becky and Elaine preferred to take a secondary chute next to the California Chute. The secondary chute offered excellent skiing ideally suited to their skill level—an important safety consideration for all steep-slope skiing.

Gary and I both wanted to be the first down through that deep untracked powder. Would it be the same if I went second? My musing ended abruptly as Gary announced: "It's yours, Glenn, go ahead; I'll be right behind you." I couldn't do that, but before I could finish my sentence thanking him and urging him to lead the way and leave me some good snow, he was gone. After two of his turns, I started, and about 40 seconds later we were at the bottom, admiring Becky and Elaine as they skied the secondary chute like pros.

We all looked up at our tracks, breathing deeply, having an appreciation of the steep! Indeed, it was steep to look down, steep to ski, but even steeper when you looked back up at it. I don't think it's melodramatic of me to say that I still feel the California Chute in my body to this day. I can change the skis and boots, but the feeling of that day will be a part of me forever.

→

In some ways, Melissa Corey Peak will remain the powerful mountain we tamed, yet the nagging thought remains that maybe our success was that the mountain permitted us to ski it that day. You know, the mountain always wins, and it is always the mountain that gives us our best runs—that run down the California Chute and all those other runs that will follow it.

—Glenn Lubbe

Good Edge Control

From a countered position, it is easy to form a platform in the snow beneath your skis that gives you stability and edge control. Create a platform by standing over the center of your skis, knees and ankles flexed, with the inside edge of your downhill ski and outside edge of your uphill ski set firmly in the snow. This instant of edging control is called an *edge set*. When accompanied by a blocking pole-plant, the edge set creates the three-point platform crucial to skiing the steeps. In fact, in steep corridors or chutes, you must think platform after platform, turn after turn.

Figure 5.4 A good edge set and proper angulation provide balance and control in steep terrain.

Try to ski the edges of both skis effectively, keeping most of your weight on the inside edge of the downhill ski as it grips the snow. Angle your outside hip and knee into the hill (this is called *angulation*). Edge the uphill ski on its outside edge with just enough pressure to give you balance and control over both of your skis (see figure 5.4). Not using angulation and a countered upper body can cause (1) inclining or leaning into the hill, with the likelihood of your edges breaking loose and your skis slipping down the hill out of control; (2) a lack of balance; (3) a lack of versatility and turning power; and (4) a lack of speed control.

Angulation and Separation

The preceding discussions have illustrated skiing situations where angulation (the action of forming an angle) and separation of the upper and lower body are crucial to accomplishing the skill. Angulation affects the edging and pressure that you apply to your skis and, ultimately, speed control and maneuverability, and is essential to steep-slope skiing. Generally, we refer to upper and lower body separation with the line of demarcation being your midsection just above the hips, because it is at this point that angles created between the upper and lower body most strongly affect ski control.

Angulation is apparent in the formation of pre-turns, where the ankles and knees are angled into the hill, as are the hip and spine. In quick edge sets or platforms, there may be only ankle and knee angulation, but in the steeps there is probably ankle, knee, hip, and spine angulation.

You can test the effect of angulation by practicing medium-radius turns on groomed steep terrain. In a medium-radius turn you predominantly ride your downhill or outside ski, applying foot and ankle pressure through the angles created by your ankle, knee, and hip as they press or flex forward and into the mountain. Flex and pressure the downhill ski gradually until the end of the turn, where there is a brief point at which you become compact (a point of maximum pressure/flexion in your skis and legs). Once the ski is released, you will deflect or rebound slightly in the direction of the next turn from the energy that had built up in the skis.

The momentum of your upper body travels directly over the end of the old turn to the center of the new turn. Work independently from foot to foot and leg to leg: as one foot increases pressure, the other relaxes until it must apply pressure, at which time the foot that was previously working decreases its pressure.

Skis have technical characteristics that enable you to ski them independently and with different pressures throughout turning. Of particular importance is a ski's camber, which equally distributes the skier's weight (pressures) over the entire length of the ski, and which gives the ski sensitivity at its ends for turning, stability, and holding. Your skis can flex in several different directions. In the medium-radius turn, you can really sense what ski design is all about, and with today's hourglass design, the quick turning of skis will improve angulation skills in the steeps.

Use your angles to add precision to the shape of your turns. To begin a long-radius turn, you may angle your outside hip into the mountain to influence the edging of your turning ski. As the turn progresses, and you begin subtly steering your inside ski, you can tighten the arc of the turn by angling your outside knee into the turn, thus increasing the amount of edging on your downhill ski. If you want a crisp end to the turn, angle your ankle into the turn to complete the edging of your turning ski, while steering both feet to finish the arc of the turn (see figure 5.5).

To shorten the radius of the turn, instead of angling the hip into the mountain first, move your knee in along with more active inside ski steering (see figure 5.6). This way, you can steer your ski to edge more quickly. With the hourglass ski design, the effect of this subtle angulation is tremendous. Regardless of design, when steered onto an edge, skis insist on turning!

Here is an exercise for groomed terrain. You may use the steeps if you are comfortable with them, but be forewarned that some aspects of this exercise can produce very fast speeds. You may want to go to a gentler slope. Ski to a place where you can safely stop, out of the way of other skiers yet still on the slope. Pick up some speed and make three turns angling first your hip, then knee, then ankle. Next make three turns angling first your knee and then your ankle. The difference is huge, because angling in your hip alone is not enough to get your turning ski onto its edge without the aid of distance. On the other hand, angling the knee will quickly set your turning ski on edge, and in a much shorter distance. Take the same run and, without stopping, make a series of turns in which you go from hip angle to knee angle to ankle angle, and back to knee angle, then hip angle.

Use knee and ankle angles in the steeps if you feel you are traveling a bit too fast. As a rule, knee angulation (knee-in) creates sharper turns; hip angulation (hip-in) creates turns with a longer radius (see figure 5.7). To tighten a medium-radius turn, check your speed or

Figure 5.5 Ankle angulation.

Figure 5.6 Ankle and knee angulation.

Figure 5.7 Ankle, knee, and hip angulation.

move to a shorter radius or short-swing turn, get on the edges very quickly, and angle the knee. In actuality, you use many angles to turn and to subtly change aspects of the turns. Use the rule on knee and hip angulation only as a guide.

When you create a long-radius turn, all the processes of a medium-radius turn are slowed down. The hip goes in more slowly and gradually. You progressively tip the ski onto its edge. For tighter turns in the steeps, your knee is angled in. To radically create angles for extremely tight turns in the steeps, however, get your hip as close to the hillside as possible with your uphill leg very short and your downhill leg fully extended and long, with your ski edged in the snow.

Strong Short-Radius Turn

We have addressed the basic skills necessary to execute short-radius turns, except quick feet, covered at length in Chapter 6 on moguls, where the skill is even more critical. You need good, solid technical skills and mental resolve to turn quickly in the steeps. It is more common in the steeps than in the moguls for skills to fall apart soon after a skier "frights-up" on the slope.

There are key mechanics to the short-radius turn in the steeps:

1. Begin the turn with a slight pre-turn platform.
2. Face down the hill with hands, arms, head, chest, and shoulders.
3. Stand tall to begin turns.
4. Project the upper body down the hill and into the turn as you uncoil at the waist—this is a "free-fall" sensation your head and body must expect and accept.
5. As you complete the turn across the hill sink into the hill by angling your ankles, knees, hips, and spine as needed—this will create an edge set and platform.
6. Plant your downhill pole as you set your edges, check your speed, and prepare to launch into your next turn (return to #2 in this sequence).

SKIING CORNICES

Before adding cornices to your skiing repertoire, consider these elements: safety, your skiing ability, the length of drop, the run-out, slope traffic, and the texture of the snow.

Safety

Is the cornice "in bounds" at a ski resort, and is it posted as open? Is access to the cornice marked and cleared? If so, avalanche control probably has been completed. However, never assume that a cornice is absolutely safe, though "reasonably safe" is a good bet given the open sign.

Not all cornices are posted, so rely on your investigation and preparation. First, if the snow is new-fallen and wet or thick, the cornice may be risky. Second, if the cornice is firm and hard, the snow beneath it may be too firm and hard for a safe landing. Third, if portions of the cornice appear cracked or to have broken away, stay away.

Skills

Can you make a short-radius turn? Can you execute a quick edge set and breaking action? Can you carry speed under control and turn on command? Do you have a reliable pole-plant that breaks your upper body's momentum? Are you comfortable looking down steep terrain that affords your skis only a quarter-inch to a half-inch of edging to hold you on the slope? "Yes" to all of these indicates that you are ready for a full variety of cornice skiing. "No" to any of the above does not necessarily rule out cornice skiing, but suggests that you should choose your cornices carefully.

Length of the Drop

The distance you travel from the top of a cornice to the snow below must be considered before leaping. To veteran leapers, a drop of 5 to 10 feet is no big deal, but when it increases to 10 to 20 feet and more, jitters can adversely affect your safety.

Be sure about it. The length of a drop affects people differently. Weigh the distance of the drop against your comfort level and cornice leaping experience to ensure that you will be relaxed when you hit the snow below (see figure 5.8).

Nature of the Run-Out

The run-out is the portion of the slope below the cornice landing area that begins to flatten out, although the flattening may be little more than a transition from very steep to steep terrain. Some run-outs are tens of feet long, although most are hundreds of yards in length. You

© Mountain Stock/Hank deVre

Figure 5.8 Leap only when you feel comfortable in your ability to ski the run-out.

should know the look and nature of the run-out before leaping and feel confident in your ability to ski its condition.

Slope Traffic

Slope traffic affects your safety. Look at what skiers below you are doing. Are they chewing up the landing sites, making them dangerously unstable? Are skiers crashing after their landings? Are skiers below the cornice skiing across the run-out? Are skiers gawking at leapers becoming obstacles to the leapers? Can skiers beneath you see leapers coming, and is there a way to let others know that you are about to leap?

Some of these concerns are not an issue on most cornices, but as hills become more crowded and grooming machines ascend the summits of more mountains, good cornices may become traffic hazards. Be aware of slope traffic; look before you leap!

Snow Texture

Great snow does not necessarily mean great cornice skiing if you are lacking the elements discussed previously in this section. Even though a veteran may say that great snow equals a great day, beginner and novice cornice skiers should pay more attention to safety and skill preparation, and consider great snow a bonus. No cornice skiing should be done unless skiers possess the skills and good sense to do it safely.

BEGINNING CORNICE SKIING

Approach cornices with a three- to six-foot drop by positioning yourself to ski off the cornice such that you can ease yourself into the slope conditions. This will give you the feeling of actually falling and reuniting with the snow below you.

At first, the angle you choose for leaving the cornice should not put you directly down the fall line. Ski off the cornice in a fan progression of different angles, starting with the shallowest (most acute) angle and increasing the angle gradually until you are skiing in the fall line (see figure 5.9). This will help you get to know the cornice and ensuing terrain. Think of every angle of descent as represented by the rib of a fan, your goal being to ski the middle portion of the fan where the rib is straight: the fall line, where you can point your skis straight down the hill and make turns to the bottom. The fan progression builds confidence as you learn to control your speed on the steep terrain below the cornice.

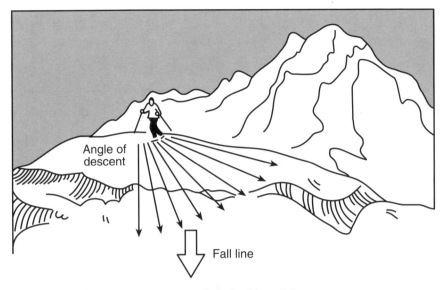

Figure 5.9 A fan progression can help build confidence.

As you increase your confidence in skiing cornices, consider adding another dimension to your fan progression: a more aggressive takeoff. Once you are comfortable going off the cornice, move farther back and pick up more speed before getting to the edge. Do this repeatedly until you sense a little spring in your legs and feet when you leap off the cornice. The spring action prevents the tails of your skis from dragging over the cornice. Once you have added spring to your leap and feel comfortable with the conditions in which you land, you will experience the exhilaration of cornice skiing.

After you leap off and land, the first turn will be out of the fall line to check your speed and establish a platform, followed by a series of rhythmic platforms and turns. The fan progression takes time and some cornices take more than a few minutes to reach (many require hiking). Plan to spend a day at it, especially the first time.

KEYS TO HIGH PERFORMANCE

1. When skiing the steeps you need a blend of edging skills, a blocking pole-plant, and an aggressive attitude.
2. Think platform when skiing the steeps: platform after platform, turn after turn, especially when you are required to make short turns in a corridor or chute.

3. Look down the hill, and ski to that point. There is no room for hesitation in very steep chutes.

4. Plant the downhill pole to block the momentum of your upper body and to enable you to set your skis' edges. In this position, your body is coiled and ready to extend down the hill and into the fall line to execute the turn. As you uncoil, you will experience a full range of up-out-down motion during this very brief midpoint of your turn; coil or sink again to set your edges for the next platform. Use subtle steering to control your transitions between full extension and your new platform, and more dramatic steering when turns must be shorter and very precise (when skiing a steep chute).

5. In the steeps, the mountain gives you momentum. Keep the momentum going for more effortless skiing; constantly allow your momentum to work for you, and use your rhythmic extension and flexion motion to create platform after platform down the fall line.

6. Static skiing in the steeps leads to timidity, leaning back, locking the knees and hips, and using the poles too little or not at all—in other words, dangerous skiing.

7. As a rule, knee angulation (knee-in) creates sharper turns; hip angulation (hip-in) creates turns with a longer radius. When you create a very long-radius turn, the processes of a medium-radius turn are slowed down.

8. On the groomed steep slope, keep the skis in contact with the snow.

9. The pole-touch rhythm becomes an internal rhythm.

10. The way to approach cornices with a three- to six-foot drop is not to jump off the particular cornice area where you're standing, but to position yourself to ski off the cornice to ease yourself into the slope conditions.

11. If you want to ski off cornices, but are unsure of yourself, use the fan progression.

12. With beginning cornice skiing, your first turn after leaping off and landing will be a pre-turn out of the fall line to check your speed and establish the platform from which your turns will follow in a series of rhythmic platforms and turns.

CHAPTER 6

MASTERING THE MOGULS

Looking for moguls rather than avoiding them indicates an appetite for adventurous and challenging skiing. A good part of mogul skiing involves attitude and perspective. Overcoming mental barriers allows your body to move fluidly in response to tactile, auditory, and visual stimuli. Skiing bumps involves reacting and responding to the feel of the snow and terrain. Approach the bumps with enjoyment.

A good attitude helps keep you in the right frame of mind to learn to ski moguls, but attitude alone is not enough. The skills and tactics for skiing the bumps are often best learned on packed runs and then taken into the bumps, or are practiced in the bumps as specific drills or tasks. Going into mogul fields repeatedly to learn to ski the bumps, when you end up merely surviving them, is likely to teach you more about your endurance and strength than about efficiently skiing moguls.

Two obstacles for many would-be bump skiers are a fear of injury and a desire not to look like a fool, both common in athletic endeavors that present a degree of risk to limb or self-esteem. There are several ways to remedy these obstacles. Some skiers gain confidence by focusing on their basic skills in the moguls and viewing the terrain as just more bumpy. Other skiers rely on psychological "self-talk" ploys to ease their minds. Some use relaxation techniques, while others explore new bump-skiing techniques and strategies by taking classes or working with skilled teachers.

Whatever your disposition, you need to address both your mental perspective toward the bumps and the skills you use to ski them. Thinking of learning to ski bumps as an adventure is one way to add enjoyment to moguls. With an adventurous attitude you can begin applying your skills to small bumps and build toward the size of bump you find most enjoyable, yet still challenging, for your level of skiing.

BARE ESSENTIALS FOR MOGUL SKIING

There are at least four areas that contribute to a successful day in the moguls: good snow, a steady head, good fitness, and playfulness.

Good Snow

Good snow depends on the type of mogul skiing you prefer. On fairly steep terrain, three to four inches of new-fallen snow blanketing nicely rounded moguls is ideal. Other favorable conditions for mogul skiing include soft spring snow on steep terrain; moguls carved out of newly fallen snow on a firm base; widely spaced moguls on moderately steep terrain with snow that is firmly packed but provides edge grip; steep terrain with tightly spaced moguls buried beneath 18 to 30 inches of new-fallen snow; and erratically spaced moguls on packed new snow that is both forgiving and cold.

Nasty snow conditions include hard, icy moguls; chopped-up frozen spring moguls; erratic moguls on very steep terrain or, even worse, erratic moguls that are frozen over; and heavy, wet powder covering any kind of bump on intermediate terrain.

Steady Head

A steady thought process and focus are essential while skiing the bumps. It is important to keep doubt and hesitancy from jeopardizing your performance.

Good Fitness

To ski bumps well for extended periods, your level of fitness specific to moguls is critical. Pay particular attention to your abdominals; quads; hamstrings; ankle, knee, and wrist joints; hips; shoulders; and hand-grip. There is a greater need for cardiovascular endurance for bump skiing than for most other alpine skiing endeavors.

(continued)

Figure 6.1, a-d Get up on the mogul, block your upper body with a pole plant, and extend to turn on the side of the mogul and through the trough.

c

d

Figure 6.1 a-d *(continued)*

Playfulness

The argument to include playfulness among the bare essentials is one that comes from years of watching people learn to ski moguls, a learning experience that many classify as their most protracted and frustrating. On frustrating days in the moguls your best coach is your laughter and playfulness.

HIGH-PERFORMANCE SKILLS

Many skills are involved in skiing moguls. You will apply these skills differently depending on the conditions. Following are several specific skills to develop in order to enhance your versatility in the moguls.

Blocking Pole-Plant

To master the moguls, you have to be able to use a pole-plant to control the speed of your upper body's movement downhill. When in the moguls, you must keep your upper body from adversely affecting the momentum of your lower body. The blocking pole-plant is executed when you reach down the hill to the top or side of the mogul to plant your pole almost perpendicular to the midline of your upper body as it faces down the fall line. The blocking pole-plant establishes a momentary slowing to allow you to complete one turn while instantly setting up for a new turn (see figure 6.1, a-d).

Quick Feet

The ability to hop from ski to ski, and quickly lift and redirect both skis at the same time, is essential to bump skiing success. You need quick feet to complement basic ski steering and turning skills. Quick feet may be inherited, but you can learn to move quickly on your skis in moguls when you perfect your basic skills and think less.

Retraction

To lighten the pressure on your skis and give you greater turning and maneuvering options in moguls, retract, or pull, your knees and quads toward your chest. Retraction allows you to neutralize the unevenness of the terrain while maintaining balance, thereby increasing your skill in the moguls (see figure 6.2, a-d).

(continued)

Figure 6.2, a-d Retract your knees to absorb the mogul.

c

d

Figure 6.2, a-d *(continued)*

A Memory of Moguls

It's been 50 years since my parents first put me on a pair of hickory skis and sent me down a snow-covered hill to my destiny. Moguls have always been a part of that destiny for me, although I also love the other variations on the theme of turning on snow. I've been racing since I was a child. I love powder, corn, glaciers, glades, and steeps. These have always been part of my enjoyment of the sport, but my favorite has always been mogul skiing.

I grew up skiing in the era before grooming—when if you wanted to ski anything steep after the first few days following a storm, you skied the huge human-made bumps that countless similar turns had forged into the hillside. As a teenager, my skis were 220 centimeters long and made of ash or hickory or some other equally easily broken substance. For much of my early life, in fact, I skied with tips reattached by epoxy cement. During the '50s if I missed a turn amid the metaphorical Volkswagen buses parked down Gunbarrel at Heavenly Valley, I was sure to break the ski tips once again as I was catapulted into an involuntary bouncy traverse.

As a still relatively young man in the '70s, when skis shortened and likewise did the bumps, I learned the different line of dogging, feet forward to absorb the unpredictably jagged edge of these new moguls and hands spread wide to quicken the pole-plants.

I still had a back in those days, and knees. Now, I am told, one side of my pelvis stands higher than the other. My knees collapse sometimes in the simple act of climbing stairs. I am also somewhat short for my weight, according to the table physicians use. I still like to ski moguls, though.

The secret—if there is a secret—to skiing moguls has remained the same for the last 50 years. In part, it's the same secret you use to ski powder, ice, steeps—you name it. It starts with a good, solid, effortless, short-radius turn. This turn has to incorporate everything your PSIA-certified instructor has told you: an early crossover into each new turn that is timed by a rhythmical pole swing, the momentary stabilization of that crossover with the pole touch, an instinctive leveraging of the ski from front to back during the turn, a ski that is steered smoothly from one turn to the next, and so on. Some—perhaps most—skiers think they are capable of just such turns on today's manicured slopes.

Something happens to them, though, when they try to carry this beautiful turn into the moguls. It disintegrates. They hang back and lose the early crossover. The pole swing and touch becomes a stab. Each turn becomes an agony of effort as they try to will the skis around too quickly to complete the turn. Their instinctive leveraging of the skis to relieve pressure is lost. The turn has lost its wholeness. It has lost its art. The lungs sear, the knees burn, the back is ready for the Jacuzzi.

→

Another part of the skill of mogul skiing is the line. There are as many different lines as there are skiers willing to ski them. Some lines require 16-year-old body parts—which, by the way, don't last forever. Other lines follow the least resistance. All are decided by the location of the pole touch. Though line is an essential part of skiing moguls, it is not the most important part.

You have to know that your body can ski moguls. You have to have faith in your skill. Perhaps that is what makes skiing so enjoyable for so many years. Skiing is an art, the rudiments of which are perfected over years of practice. When you know that you are an artist—when you believe in yourself—you gain the confidence to brush that art all over a hillside of bumpy snow. Your self-confidence becomes a self-fulfilling prophecy, and you are a mogul skier, even when youth is a foggy memory, one leg is shorter than the other, and the knees collapse while rising from a couch.

—Tony Roegiers

Ski Feel

You need to be aware of the texture of the mogul's snow, the steepness of the terrain, the hardness of the troughs, and the overall density of the mogul field (e.g., are the moguls long and rhythmic, short and erratic, or smooth and round?). Ski feel is the skier's information conduit.

Upper and Lower Body Separation

Your lower body has to be able to direct and redirect itself independent of your upper body, which is maintaining a posture that positions it square to the fall line. The upper body is a stable mass moving downhill, permitting the lower body to adapt beneath it as needed to effect a smooth movement through the bumps.

Good upper and lower body separation creates the dynamic tension that adds rotary power to the lower body when it twists opposite the upper body while turning or negotiating a "quick foot" maneuver in the bumps.

Disciplined Short-Radius and Short-Swing Turns

Your success in the moguls depends on your ability to make disciplined short-radius and short-swing turns. The short-radius turn is made quickly, but has an arc or carve to it (even though there may be some skidding). The short-radius turn effects travel down the slope for a relatively short distance (10 to 20 feet).

A short-swing turn is also made quickly, although the tails of the skis fan or sweep along the snow to effect a very short distance of travel (essentially a couple of feet farther than the length of the skis). Mogul skiers use both styles of short turn depending on the conditions and configuration of the mogul field, and should be proficient in both.

Practice short-radius and short-swing turns on smooth terrain, and then take them into the bumps. A drill you may try just for fun is to start a series of rhythmic short-radius or short-swing turns on smooth terrain that leads into an easy mogul field. As you ski into the mogul field, see how long you can maintain the rhythm. To rev up this drill, start a rhythm in the bumps and see how long you can maintain it. In both varieties of this drill, you are skiing your rhythm first. You may find that you have to ski over, around, or even through bumps that get in the way of your rhythm. Try this for both types of short turn.

Directional Skidding

Sidestepping, skidding forward, and even skidding backward provide flexibility and versatility. All are desirable for maximum opportunity in the bumps.

Strong On-Off Edging Skills

The ability to get on and off the edges of your skis to stop, slow, or turn is essential for bump skiing. Executing an edge set and quickly releasing it is crucial to difficult bump skiing in the steeps (see figure 6.3, a and b). On–off edging skills indicate that you can use both the inside and outside edges of your skis. Complement the quick on-and-off edging with pole-plants and upper and lower body separation.

Figure 6.3, a and b Check your edges and uncoil to create a hop turn around the mogul.

STRATEGIES FOR SKIING MOGULS

Skiers approach moguls in many ways. They ski the tops of the bumps, the troughs between the bumps, or the fronts, sides, or backs of the bumps. You can ski any combination of the above on any run. Depending on the shape and height of the moguls, the snow conditions, the terrain, and your energy level, you will want to use every option open to you. Keep the enjoyment theme in mind and realize that, rather than one perfect way to ski moguls, there are many ways to approach the bumps by using various skills and bump skiing strategies.

Think of the Ride

The essence of turning in the bumps is momentarily steering both skis to the position on a bump where you want to turn, and then following through by actually steering your skis into your turn. *Ride* the moguls: perhaps by you extending your downhill leg to establish dominance of your turning (carving) ski while continuing to steer your resting uphill ski through the turn; perhaps by riding them both evenly; or by guiding one ski on the side of a bump while the downhill ski is riding through the trough.

In the latter example, as one leg works, the other rests, until the instant when both skis momentarily meet to be guided into the next turn. In effect, *guide* briefly with both skis, and *ride* the downhill ski through the bumps.

Know the Snow's Texture and Shape of the Moguls

Use the top part of the mogul run to get a feel for the snow. As you traverse the run, retract (suck up) your legs to absorb the top of the moguls and to focus on the snow's texture and its resistance against your skis. Assess the resistance against your skis as you extend your legs into the troughs between moguls. If the going is too slow and cumbersome, angle your traverse more downhill to maintain momentum.

Explore Dynamic Movements

Continue to traverse while hopping off the tops of moguls and extending your legs into the troughs so that you blast through the loose snow likely to be there. When you are on top of the moguls, point your skis away from where you want to go. Begin your turns by hopping and then turning your skis in the air. Travel through the loose

Figure 6.4 Keep your skis in control for your landing.

snow in the trough, landing on both skis as you fully complete the turn (see figure 6.4). Do this until you feel ready to point your skis more down the fall line, and then continue randomly with the hopping and turning. This hopping drill will add aggressiveness to your mogul skiing.

Know How to Handle Windblown Snow Between Moguls

This is a special mogul skiing situation. There are several problems with windblown snow and moguls. One is psychological. You can't see the trough or the depth of the loose snow. The mogul is likely to be firm and the trough soft. This creates resistance in the trough as well as a significant change in conditions when skiing between mogul and trough.

Too often, skiers ski straight at these moguls without making a turn. By the time they get to the trough, they are carrying too much speed and react by turning through the trough. However, the resistance in the soft snow deflects the skis, and some skiers are thrown in toward the mountain.

If, however, you are well into your turn as you enter the trough, you have already engaged the strongest part of your rotary skill to take you through the trough. The skis brush the loose snow out of the way and spray it downhill. If you wait too long to turn (if you begin your turn in the trough) you will run into trouble.

It is important to keep skis hip-width apart rather than pasted together so that they can be worked independently. Using this stance, try this exercise: open the tails of the skis to form a very narrow, short-leg, long-leg wedge. Your downhill leg is longer than your uphill leg; the uphill leg is bent and pulled in slightly for balance as it would be if you were walking across a steep hill.

In a short-leg, long-leg wedge turn, there is a pinching in the waist (on the long-leg side of your body) similar to the feel when doing side bends, and pressure on both skis. As you turn through windblown snow between the moguls, turn with your downhill (long-leg) ski and give your uphill (short-leg) ski a nice, smooth line through the snow that your downhill ski has brushed away. Turning this way allows the downhill leg to work while the uphill leg rests. The uphill ski is guided through the turn with less pressure even though it may be riding along the side of the mogul. Such is the rhythm of mogul skiing: the downhill ski works while the uphill ski rides, back and forth, leg to leg, with no lag between. This is independent leg action.

REVVING UP YOUR PERFORMANCE IN THE BUMPS

There are more than a few ways to rev up your performance in the bumps, and the following will discuss some of these. But before going out to work on your mogul skiing skills it's important to acknowledge that your commitment to revving up your bump skiing is the first important step toward accomplishing this goal. With this in mind, each incremental gain will have relevance to your skiing.

Anticipation

As your skis extend into a trough, look down the fall line (see figure 6.5, a and b). Plant the pole and cast the weight of your upper body

Figure 6.5, a and b Keep your body in proper alignment and look ahead.

in the direction of the next turn; your skis will follow. Anticipate each subsequent turn all the way down the slope. By using upper and lower body separation, you stabilize your speed, increase your ease of turning, and turn early. Keep your body in proper alignment to improve your balance and force yourself to keep looking ahead.

Retraction and Extension

Retraction and extension are used to neutralize the bumps, allowing your upper body to move along as if the bumps weren't even there. It is not easy to incorporate this into your skiing, yet when retraction–extension becomes automatic, you have a powerful force working for you on the mountain in all conditions. Practice retraction–extension in your free skiing and eventually it will join you in the bumps.

An exercise you can use to work on retraction–extension in your free skiing is *prejumping* knolls or natural terrain jumps. Instead of blasting over knolls or natural terrain jumps, use them as opportunities to retract and extend. Just before you reach the takeoff point, retract your knees, keeping your skis in as much contact with the snow as possible. As soon as you pass this point, fully extend your legs down the knoll to maintain contact with the snow.

Match Lines (or Make a Commitment to Turning)

There is no one perfect line through the bumps. There may be efficient lines, but even these depend on your skiing ability, strength, mood, and the snow conditions. Bump skiers who enjoy their runs take the line that they prefer, but it helps to practice other lines as well.

Try this: Stand atop a bump run and identify as many lines as you can through the bumps. Look for the most obvious lines laid by other skiers. Pick out a line that is different from how you would choose to ski this hill, and match the line by skiing it. Here's the catch: you must commit yourself to making four to six turns before stopping to assess how it felt. At this point, you can either continue matching the line for another 5 to 10 turns, or match another line for four to six turns.

Attack Bumps in a Series

Except for specific drills, when skiing bumps commit yourself to skiing a series of at least four turns or bumps; do not ski bumps one at a time. This is particularly helpful to new bump skiers faced with a half mile or more of bumps. At first, the hill may look impossible, but by breaking it into segments you not only ski better but also counter some of the intimidation of the bumps. Perceive the bumps in series of 50 to 100 feet each. As you feel more comfortable with each subsequent series, the bumps become less intimidating. Start with a four-turn commitment and build up to a 20-turn commitment.

Be Loose, Flexible, and Fluid

If, while skiing the bumps, you find yourself thinking a lot about technique rather than just skiing, you are working too hard. Drills are for thinking; bump skiing requires being loose, flexible, and fluid. You must be reactional and rely on the skills that you have perfected through drills and free skiing.

Establish Rhythm (and Build Confidence)

The fear of losing control in the bumps keeps many skiers from skiing them at all. You can avoid losing control by establishing a rhythm. Whether your skiing is slow and deliberate or goofy and loose, you can enjoy the bumps when you are skiing in control.

Keep Your Arms Forward

In the bumps, proper upper body alignment means that your arms are forward and facing down the fall line (see figure 6.6, a-c). Your arms should be away from your body and out ahead of you, not hanging aimlessly at your sides or dangling behind you, pulling and tugging your upper body back into the hill.

Freestyle and Other Approaches to the Bumps

There are many ways to ski the bumps. The perspective presented in this chapter is based on concepts learned from World Cup racing techniques and refinements of less aggressive methods. Freestyle bump skiers are a breed in themselves, blasting down bump runs for speed with a few aerials thrown in for effect. Some recreational skiers try to mimic this acrobatic style of bump skiing, despite too little experience, too little strength, and poor reactional skills, and many of these skiers get injured.

Other ways to ski bumps include swiveling the skis on the top of one bump, sliding through the troughs and up to the top of another bump without making any clearly defined turns, skiing bump to bump by bouncing off the tops of the bumps, or skiing bump to bump by banking off the sides of the bumps.

a

b

(continued)

Figure 6.6, a-c   Keep your arms in front, your head up, and use your angles to ski the bumps.

c

Figure 6.6, a-c *(continued)*

KEYS TO HIGH PERFORMANCE

1. Mogul skiing is part attitude and perspective. Your attitude about the bumps keeps you in the right frame of mind to learn to ski them.

2. There is more than one way to ski moguls, and there are several skills you should develop to enhance your versatility in the bumps.

3. Ski moguls by retracting your legs when on top of the mogul and extending your legs into the trough of the upcoming mogul.

4. Ski moguls with independent leg action and dynamic turning.

5. Ski moguls with a rhythm—one ski works while the other rides, back and forth, leg to leg.

6. The new turn begins as soon as you have stood on the ski that is turning you; while the uphill ski is guided it is actually being set up to make the next turn.

7. Two obstacles for many would-be bump skiers are fear of injury and fear of looking like a fool. To most recreational skiers, moguls look like obstacles. Do not ski a difficult run until you are technically ready. Practice applying basic skills in comfortable terrain and gradually work up to more challenging terrain. Most recreational skiers don't get enough skiing time to develop expert mogul skills. Patience, along with the commitment to spend part of your skiing time doing drills and exercises in the bumps, will improve both your overall skiing and your proficiency in the bumps.

CHAPTER 7

POWDER SKIING

There is something wonderful about skiing in snow where you cannot see your skis, boots, or even legs. Skiing effortlessly through light, new-fallen powder is a compelling dream. However, some good yet inexperienced powder skiers find the deep stuff very intimidating. Powder skiing is momentum skiing down the fall line, but unless a different application of basic skiing skills is applied, being unable to see your skis will likely spell t-r-o-u-b-l-e.

BARE ESSENTIALS
FOR POWDER SKIING

There are several elements that are basic to powder skiing. Some are predictors of a better powder day than others, but all are important to consider.

Terrain Appropriate to the Texture of the Powder

Given the right pitch of descent, most textures of powder can be a treat. Combine heavy, wet powder with a slight pitch, however, and you have problems if you need to cover some distance in a reasonable period of time. Terrain is important when choosing your powder runs: the deeper the snow, the steeper the pitch that's needed is a good rule. Fluffy light snow can be skied easily on steep terrain as well as on terrain with lesser degrees of pitch.

Some Measure of Abandon

A glimpse of powder skiers out there hootin' and hollerin' as they rip up the mountain indicates their level of "white eye" insanity. These skiers take with them an attitude of abandon—but not recklessness or bravado—when they dive into one powder run after another. Skiers who have an attitude of abandon view powder as an inviting adventure instead of an intimidating challenge (see figure 7.1).

Appropriate Attire (Including Eyewear)

The wrong attire can cancel the outstanding potential for a day in the powder. Your attire is very important when you consider the difference it can make to both your safety and a great day in the powder.

© Mountain Stock/Chaco Mohler

Figure 7.1 View powder as an inviting adventure instead of an intimidating challenge.

When skiing powder during storms, on windy days, or in the trees, goggles are a necessity. On sunny days with ego fluff powder in open bowls and sweeping trails a well-fitted pair of sunglasses will suffice.

Good Fitness

Powder skiing can be physically demanding. If you already have powder skills, a high level of ski fitness may translate into a long carefree day in the powder. If you are learning powder skills, a high level of ski fitness helps your endurance and your progress toward skill development.

Appropriate Skis

What are the best skis for powder? Before making your decision, consider a condensed history of modern powder skiing:

In the '70s, flexible giant slalom skis were every ski bum's designated powder skis. In the '80s, along came dynamic powder skiers who took their broader-tipped slalom skis right from the race course to the powder without a hitch. Prior to the fatter skis of the '90s, a lot of ski instructors noticed that the best powder skis for students were the skis they felt most comfortable skiing.

When "fat boys" first hit the slopes, the mainstream ski manufacturers chuckled, some ski instructors thought, "Oh boy, another gimmick," and the powder purists scoffed. Now wide powder boards are captivating ski instructors and skiers alike who line up to sample the latest "fat" powder skis from their favorite mainstream ski manufacturers.

In 1995, for the first time, all of the teams (including the U.S. team) competing in the World Pairs Powder Skiing Championships used "fat" powder skis. The recent explosion of snowboarding has broadened the definition of powder hounds, and the standard "two-board" hounds are fast becoming the minority in the trees and open bowls, sharing terrain with boarders, powder board skiers, and of late, skiers on shaped skis.

Before you buy skis, try the "fat" powder skis. They are broad, soft in flex, and are generally used in shorter lengths than all-mountain skis (e.g., 175 to180 centimeters for men of average height, weight, and skill; 160 to 165 centimeters for women of average height, weight, and skill). Shaped skis are also solid performers in powder and are, like "fat" skis, used in shorter lengths without sacrificing performance.

Powder purists continue to ski powder, and ski it well, on slalom and giant slalom skis. There are expert skiers who also ride snowboards, and would rarely use anything but their snowboards on a good (or challenging) stormy powder day. Powder is a very personal experience, except in pairs competition, where precision, speed, coordination, and timing are critical to success.

HIGH-PERFORMANCE SKILLS

Several areas of skill development can enhance your success with powder skiing and, on perfection, can lead to your refusal to ski anything but powder—which is when you move to the mountains for good!

Dynamic Balance

The difference between *balance* and *dynamic balance* is exemplified by the difference between standing on the top of a narrow wall versus walking along the top of a narrow wall. In powder skiing, you want to feel relaxed and confident moving along the top of the narrow wall.

Dynamic balance is innate or can be developed with practice. You can develop your dynamic balance by repeated experimental acquaintance runs in 5- to 10-inch deep powder. Ski down a gentle slope, skis together, to get the feeling of these three characteristics of powder: texture, depth, and resistance against your skis (see figure 7.2). Also assess your balance point (where you stand on your skis). Try to center yourself over both skis, balancing yourself as much as possible. Be very deliberate about this so that you are moving along in balance with your skis, the snow, and the terrain. Relax your upper body to encourage your lower body to adjust appropriately while developing its dynamic balance.

To accentuate this development, add retraction–extension movements to your skiing; at first make rapid movements, then slow them down and make them more subtle. When you look back at your tracks in the snow they may show areas of greater compression from your extension and areas of less compression from your retraction. Repeat this several times until you become so used to the powder's characteristics that you feel relaxed. Then change slopes and conditions and repeat the exercise.

Foot and Lower-Leg Steering

Turning precisely on groomed or powder slopes begins with your feet and lower legs directing your skis into the distinct beginning of

© David Stocklein

Figure 7.2 Consciously retract your skis in the powder.

your turns, and ends with them subtly bringing you out of your turns. Practice out of the powder until your turns are very defined and controlled. Then bring these turns into the powder.

As you progress through the retraction–extension exercise described above, concentrate on feeling (in your feet and lower legs) your skis as they are retracted up and extended down. The down motion of your legs will create a type of platform beneath your skis. In powder, the goal is to feel like your skis and the snow are doing the work together: retracting and extending in *dynamic balance*. As you consciously retract your skis, the snow will project them up toward the surface where they will have less resistance and be easier to turn (see figure 7.3).

You can experiment by adding some basic rotary movements (i.e., the simultaneous pivoting of both skis). As you practice, you will grow more comfortable with the characteristics of the powder and you will be ready to approach a more challenging fall line and actually turn your skis. Pick a place in the trees that looks open. Begin retraction–extension movements. As you retract your legs, add a rotary movement by pivoting both skis together in the direction of your next turn. As you extend your legs, continue steering both feet

Figure 7.3 In powder, pole use rhythm is a key high-performance skill.

through the completion of your turn, letting your momentum counter the resistance the snow will exert against your boots and skis at this point. Then retract again with a new turn accomplished through rotary movement of your lower legs and feet.

Pole-Use Rhythm

Powder skiers use the pole-touch and the pole-swing primarily as timing devices. Because speed control is so important in powder, pole-use rhythm is a key high-performance skill for the powder skier (see figure 7.4).

Blocking pole-plants are not productive in powder, but swinging the poles and touching the tips in the powder coordinate the other key elements of turning, one of which is the steering action of your feet and lower legs.

To develop pole use rhythm, continue the previous exercise. Add an exaggerated pole-touch at the end of your retraction (the beginning of your new turn), and as you extend to turn, drive your knees

Figure 7.4 As you come up realign your body to the fall line.

to chase your outreached pole. Along with the extending and contracting and the lower-body steering, you will be producing slow but vigorous extended movements accompanied by light retracted rotary movements. Your pole will be used not as a brace to lean on, but as a prop that provides rhythm to your turns.

Upper and Lower Body Rotary Control

Now that your legs and feet are working together in dynamic balance, aided by your pole-use rhythm, you are ready to integrate the turning power of your entire body and apply this to more demanding powder situations. Rev up the beginning principles presented thus far.

A Day With the Hotshots

When I walked out of the locker room on a warm, sunny, fresh powder day, I received my list of students to instruct for the morning. They were the hotshots: the elite youth skiers on the way to becoming high-performance skiers. I had never skied with the hotshots before, and I wondered: Could these six-year-olds really be on the road to high-performance skiing, and could I keep them happy and entertained, and educate them, too?

All seven students were dressed in racing gear, powder pants, goggles, and helmets. We grabbed our skis and headed for the slopes. We warmed up with a beginner run. We did some stretches and a little game of "Simon Says." From the beginning, I knew this class was going to be special. All of my students rode up the chairlift and got off with no problems. I couldn't help smiling as I watched my seven prodigies work so hard doing their stretches, all of them listening and performing the stretches as instructed.

Skiing down the mountain working on bunny hops, short-radius turns, and long-radius turns, I could tell that my hotshots were bored. Although they stayed attentive and never complained, I knew they needed a little more action. I marveled at the agility and coordination of these six-year-olds as they skated toward the lift for the intermediate run.

I was sure this run would provide some challenges, and I told them to follow me down the mountain. I started off with some simple intermediate turns. When we teach children to ski, we typically use a different vocabulary. For example, I asked the kids to make "pie turns" followed by "railroad tracks" (wedge turns into parallel turns) to work on coordination and steering. As I was talking I heard a few giggles, and it dawned on me that these hotshots were too mature for my lingo.

After watching this group handle the intermediate run, I knew they were ready for an advanced run. I was convinced that these hotshots were on their way to becoming high-performance skiers. When we got to the top of the mountain, I was prepared to assure my class that they were safe, that it was okay to be a little scared, and to remain focused on their ability to ski, but there wasn't a peep from any of them.

I didn't need to utter a word—these six-year-olds had no fear, and they seemed ready to take on any challenge. Before we headed down the mountain, I discussed the rules. They were to follow my turns, not get too close to the skier in front of them, notify me if someone fell, keep focused, and have fun! After a few screams of excitement, I told the class they had to catch me, and we were off, racing down the mountain.

→

We skied hard the rest of the day. We covered parallel turning, steeps, balance, pole-plants, weight distribution, carved turns, edging, moguls, jumps, attitude, and control. I took the group down Skateboard Alley, a black diamond run that was narrow and covered with jumps, moguls, drop offs, and a frozen-over waterfall. The hotshots were studs, and both they and I knew it. They were definitely on their way to becoming high-performance skiers.

Youth hotshot skiers are one of the highlights in teaching kids to ski. Hotshot skiers who are attentive and disciplined are capable of skiing almost any mountain, terrain, or condition. They listen and stay focused and, most importantly, they know how to have fun. These kids know what they want for themselves, which is part of becoming a high-performance skier. One has to make the conscious decision to want to ski at a high level of performance; these six-year-olds had made this decision, and their parents and I were able to help them chase their dreams.

High-performance skiing is achievable at all ages. These six-year-olds set their minds on high-performance skiing. They were willing to take on the challenges necessary to achieve high performance in their skiing. These kids are skiing their way to the top.

—Tayesa Alexis Yacenda

1. During your retraction movements, add more emphasis to the rising and dipping of your outside ski, thereby allowing your inside ski to be lighter in the powder. In doing this, you will be more aware of the weight, pressure, and steering action of your outside ski, independent of your inside ski, in the powder. This is a dynamic approach to powder.

2. Consciously lighten your feet at the end of your down movement. As you flex down, let your feet float up slightly toward you. Although deliberate at first, these movements will soon become subtle aspects of your powder skiing.

3. Along with the rotary movements of your feet as you come up, project your hip to realign your body to the fall line—left turn, right hip; right turn, left hip. Do this by thrusting your hip to the outside and forward, allowing your body to fall diagonally down the fall line and into your next turn. This technique is particularly important on steeper runs with deeper snow.

Dynamic Leg Movement and Crossover

These skills are usually reserved for the expert powder skier who skis outrageous powder: steep, difficult, chopped, heavy, or light. This skier needs four characteristics to accomplish consistent dynamic leg movement and crossover: strength and physical conditioning; well-developed technique; plenty of experience in all kinds of powder conditions; and an aggressive and committed attitude.

An expert powder skier's leg movements are dynamic, moving laterally in and out, while the upper body remains relatively still, not twisting itself around to help turn the body but riding calmly atop a very active lower body. An expert powder skier does not ski over the skis, but moves the skis out from under him or her, their retraction and extension movements reaching side to side, turn to turn like a pendulum, creating very exciting skiing!

Selective Use of Rotational Force

Under circumstances such as very deep powder, very wet 18- to 30-inch deep powder, and wet powder on an intermediate slope, skiers may want to create rotational force to effect smooth and rhythmic turning of their skis. Rotation is the primary turning power in skiing deep powder, and at times you may want to use the upper body to boost rotation. You can do this by swinging your outside arm into the turn to help rotate your body.

As you are extending to complete a right turn, touch the left pole; as you retract to turn left, thrust your right arm (the outside arm) down the fall line to create greater rotational force on your legs, which should already have been steered left as you retracted them. After thrusting forward (downhill), swing the right arm and pole through, and as your legs extend to complete the left turn, place your right pole in the snow to initiate your next right turn, and begin to rotate the left arm down the fall line.

As you spend time in deep powder, you will become familiar with the function and necessity of rotation. You will ski with the necessary rotation without having to create it by overusing your upper body, unless conditions call for this strategy. Nevertheless, it is a powder-skiing goal to ski with your upper body separated from your lower body.

For many, the key to powder is hinging the knees together. This can apply to both the more vertical retraction and extension of the legs in beginning and advanced powder skiing or to the lateral retraction and extension in the elite powder skiing. Keeping your knees hinged, or as close together as possible, while retrieving your skis out of the snow during retraction allows you a more controlled and problem-free initiation of your new turn while simultaneously guiding your skis in the direction you want to go.

As you continue into your turn, *ride* your skis as they bend or arc through the loose snow to form a platform from the compression of the snow beneath their bases. In powder skiing with independent leg action, there are two interrelated platforms formed beneath the snow. This is true even as the knees are held close together, moving up and down to correspond to the independence of your legs.

Whether one or two platforms are formed, the critical matter is to continue to *guide* your skis throughout the turn as long as your legs are extended—particularly through (and against) the powder that is above your boots. Visualize turns in powder as continuous maneuvers: *guide* your skis into a turn, *ride* them momentarily as they form a platform in the snow, and then *guide* them to the completion of the turn. In powder as on pack, link your turns to maintain control of speed and to ensure maneuverability: steer into one turn by steering out of another.

CONQUERING HEAVY, WET POWDER

Do not spend an entire day in heavy, wet powder. You have to be more aggressive in these conditions because pushing or pressing the snow out of the way of your turning ski is going to be difficult—wet snow offers a lot of resistance. To overcome the added and unusual resistance, actively steer your knees into the hill with each retraction movement, create added rotational force, or use *leap-and-land turns.*

Begin with slight retraction and extension movements of your legs and advance to more vigorous up-and-down movements. Next, on the up side of the bounce, simultaneously turn both feet and skis to create a hopping turn. In order to use this and other exercises in heavy, wet snow, you must have a sufficiently steep slope to provide less resistance against your skis and greater momentum for turning.

The primary intention of leap-and-land turns is to lessen the resistance from the snow and use the strength in your legs to press or bend your skis through the snow into the completion of the turn. This is an active retraction–extension turn. When you retract, retract legs and feet simultaneously; as you extend, extend legs and feet with the same amount of force.

Acquaint yourself with the resistance that you will experience on a slope. First traverse the slope at different angles to feel where you are on your skis and to feel the characteristics of the snow. In this way, you develop a kinesthetic appreciation of the elements you are working with or against in heavy, wet snow. Then you can decide whether to assume an aggressive attitude and ski the conditions, or wait for another day.

If you take a positive and aggressive attitude about heavy, wet snow and become proficient in this condition, you will add to your overall skiing ability.

Another turn that works well in heavy, wet snow that is five to eight inches deep is the *uphill stem*. It is actually a skidded turn where your turning ski sets the arc of the turn and the inside ski matches it. Imagine how this kind of turn would work in difficult, hard-to-move snow. You push the turning ski out to brush away the snow, then begin steering it into the turn. While doing this, release the pressure on your new inside ski and steer it to a slightly skidded match to your turning ski. Once you become skilled with this turn, you will understand the importance of starting your turn early to establish a good base, and then completing the turn throughout its arc to maintain rhythm and control in these conditions.

POWDER SKIING ON EGO FLUFF

Ego fluff powder is three to five inches of new-fallen, dry, light snow (or medium-light snow) covering previously groomed and packed terrain. Everyone benefits from ego fluff, particularly novice powder skiers. If you are a powder novice, ego fluff is the powder to learn in. With ego fluff there are few technical nuances that you need to apply, assuming that you are already skiing confidently and efficiently.

Go out onto your favorite slope early. Ski as you normally do right down the center of the slope. If you feel that you are having some difficulty, look back at your tracks to see if they are rounded like a series of the letter S or sharp like a series of the letter Z. If they are rounded, you are skiing well. If they are sharp, you are not finishing your turns (see figure 7.5).

If the Z is apparent, return to the slope and try lengthening your turns. Ski a long- to medium-radius turn. Steer your skis through five or six turns, rounding them as much as you can by gradual pressure through the arc of the turn. Look at your new tracks. If they are

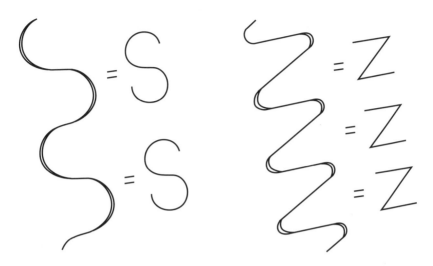

Figure 7.5 Study the shape of your turns.

rounder than before, continue to ski rounded shorter-radius turns and pick up the cadence of your skiing. Make shorter-radius turns by increasing the tempo of your pole-touch. Stay centered: don't sit back and don't lean forward. You don't have to put equal weight on both skis; stand more on your downhill ski. Touch with your poles as usual.

Enjoy this kind of snow when you can. The elements of powder that make skiing difficult are wetness, pitch, and depth. Ego fluff offers a tremendous opportunity for beginning powder skiers to practice, and for experienced packed-snow skiers to do a visual check on their overall skiing.

If you experience difficulties with ego fluff, it is possible that it is too wet or that there is too little pitch to the slope, causing too much drag on your skis. Turning ability, however, may be the reason for your difficulty. If you cannot create a rounded turn, either short- or medium-radius, on packed slopes it will be apparent in your powder tracks.

The problems you encounter in ego fluff powder are exaggerations of the problems you have on any groomed slopes. If you have technical problems with basic skiing skills, they will show up more dramatically in these conditions. Perfect your skiing on packed or groomed slopes, then head to ego fluff for your introduction to powder.

ENHANCING YOUR POWDER SKIING

Consider these items when working on your powder skills, and practice, practice, practice.

Your Power in Powder Comes From Momentum

Carry the momentum of your body down the fall line. Versatility in powder comes from your manipulation of the momentum with ankle flexion, knee steering, and hip projections by which you direct your outside hip down the fall line. Rely on your lower body to rotate while retracted and continue this rotation all the way through the extension and completion of your turn.

Take Command of the Conditions

Go into powder with the attitude that you are in charge. If you ski tentatively, you cannot derive flowing rhythmic movements. To be in charge, dictate the radii of the turns and ski with the attitude that you're lighter than the powder. Feeling light in powder will allow you to ski close to the surface because of the buoyancy of your skis.

Let Go and Experience Effortlessness

The attitude and sensation of letting go in powder complements the previous tip. Once you have worked on your powder skills, go to the powder and ski loosely. This will help you let go, and as you allow your body and mind to ski without restrictions your skiing will become effortless. Momentum and attitude will find a perfect balance.

Know How to Ski Deep, Light Powder

Dynamic skiing in slow motion is the essence of deep, light powder, and beyond the sheer ecstasy of skiing untracked snow in the trees, through open bowls, and down chutes, the quality of this experience can be addicting. For a moment, consider skiing a groomed run very smoothly and effortlessly. Your turns are crisp, rhythmic, rounded, and well-sequenced. Now imagine that same feeling in the powder, only in slow motion: nothing abrupt, nothing aggressive; you're truly flowing with the powder.

Know How to Ski Deep, Heavy Powder

Alas, not all powder is slow-motion powder. Deep, heavy powder requires aggressiveness and determination. Still, your skiing has a subtle and quiet component. For example, as you ski more aggressively you must exaggerate your pole rhythm, extension–retraction, rotary steering, and hip projection. The subtlety comes into play when you float between turns from the extended position to the retracted position. While floating, your skis cross under your stable upper body. This lightening of the skis takes the harshness out of skiing powder, and is accentuated with today's wide powder skis.

A Powder Skier is a Centered Skier

The powder skier skis over the center of the skis. You do not need to ski on your tails because your ski is designed to bend up against the force of the snow. Skiing on the tails, once a popular strategy when only stiffer and longer skis were available, puts you out of balance with the turning forces of your skis (the mid-portion) and makes powder skiing fatiguing. Some good powder skiers seem to be sitting back at times, but they are actually standing upright, square with the fall line, their skis beneath them, poised and ready to move in either direction. A centering exercise on smooth terrain is to ski with your boots unbuckled. If you don't stay centered over your skis, you will not be able to turn well or subtly control the speed of your skis.

Powder Skiing Demands Absolute Commitment

Powder skiing requires commitment to (1) the first few turns, (2) pole rhythm, (3) projection down the hill, (4) continuous movement, (5) looking ahead, (6) being in charge, (7) staying light, (8) letting go, and (9) staying in the powder and exploring the mountain. To build commitment, decide that you will make a certain number of turns in succession without stopping. Start with four turns and, as discussed with bump skiing, progress to 20 turns. Ski around the mountain and hunt up new powder adventures.

Hinge Your Knees Together

Hinge your knees together to help your lower legs and feet (skis) turn as one unit, even as your skis may be used independently (see figure 7.6).

Figure 7.6 Hinge your knees together.

KEYS TO HIGH PERFORMANCE

1. Get to know the three characteristics of powder: texture, depth, and resistance against your skis.

2. In powder, center yourself over both skis.

3. Feel your skis moving up and down: the down motion, which results from extending your legs, creates a type of platform in the snow; the up motion, which results from retracting your legs, represents the action of your skis floating through the snow.

4. Turn your skis during the up motion; complete your turn during the down motion.

5. The upper body can help to create rotation in the powder, but it is not necessary once you have perfected your powder skills. Until then, you can practice using the upper body to assist rotation by thrusting the arms down the fall line.

6. Skiing heavy, wet powder requires certain turning skills and an aggressive attitude. Two kinds of turns you can use in heavy, wet powder are the leap-and-land and the uphill stem.

7. Ego fluff provides a good opportunity to practice powder skiing. The shape of your tracks in ego fluff reveals a great deal about your skiing, including weaknesses and deficiencies in your basic skiing skills.

8. Hinge your knees together in powder, allowing them to work as a unit that is responsive to the movements of your legs and feet.

CHAPTER 8

HIGH-PERFORMANCE RACING

If you're naturally athletic and competitive, recreational, club, and league racing may light fires in you that will be difficult, if not impossible, to extinguish. There may be many more benefits to high-performance racing, as you'll discover in this chapter. Properly running gates forces you to ski more precisely and perhaps more aggressively, to use many skills, and to employ your skiing senses (e.g., sight, sound, touch, balance, proprioception) as well as your kinesthetic memory. Proper training for ski racing demands technical skill improvement and will make you a better skier.

Ask three questions if you are interested in exploring recreational racing:

- Are you good enough to begin recreational racing?
- Where will you compete?
- How will you train?

There are many forms of recreational racing and many opportunities for training once you know where to look. Most are readily available to the skiing public.

RACING BASICS

With the many different levels of recreational racing available, all skiers can find opportunities to match their skiing skills. Racing is fun, challenging, and improves your skiing skills.

Practice and Training

The first step toward preparing and improving is to get access to practice gates. For the average recreational racer the availability of gates depends on the resorts that you frequent. Although most resorts have regularly scheduled races, if you're looking for practice gates you may have to find pay-as-you-go practice courses or coin-operated courses. These are usually available to the general public several times per week. Also, most resorts have recreational racing clinics that provide expert coaching and practice gates. Check with the local ski school, race department, or local race club.

If you are looking for as many training and racing opportunities as you can find, consider adult racing camps during the season or summer ski camps. These will provide you with excellent training opportunities and an exciting vacation. Many resorts in the United States offer training programs for the local Masters and other adult racers. These may be on weekends, holidays, or evenings. Consult with the local race department or ski school.

Many would-be recreational racers are obsessed with the desire to get in the gates, despite recommendations from the pros to free ski and do training exercises and racing-related drills on the mountain. These exercises and drills are far more beneficial than learning racing techniques by banging gates on a practice course or running as many races as possible on a public course.

You must, however, run gates some of the time. There are practice courses (coin-op courses) and race courses (standard races, league races, resort races, and tour citizen races, for instance). Both practice and race courses are set by experienced course setters. Most of the courses are set on easy terrain and are user-friendly to ski.

Practice courses allow you to perform drills and experiment with different techniques at your own pace for as long as you want. Race courses are more restricted, providing you limited exposure to the gates, and usually operate on a pay-per-run basis. The advantage of the coin-op courses and National Standard Race (NASTAR) courses for practice is that they provide you with instant timing. This can be helpful in mapping progress.

Racing Opportunities

Most ski resorts offer recreational race opportunities. These are usually in the form of coin-operated courses, a local standard course, and NASTAR. NASTAR is a program run at ski areas throughout the United States. Ski areas usually have their NASTAR course set three to seven days per week. The course is open to the general public for a small fee. Courses are set on easy terrain and then run by a local pace setter who has a national handicap based on times established by U.S. Ski Team members. You will receive a time and handicap for each run; thus you can compare yourself, by handicap, to the local pace setter and the best racers in the United States. Another advantage to NASTAR's handicap system is that you can race at different resorts around the country and still monitor your skiing progress.

Club and league racing are more organized and competitive forms of recreational racing. The United States Ski Association (USSA) offers racing as yet another step to higher competition. The USSA also offers a Masters race program for skiers ages 25 through 80.

Although coin-operated race courses can be used for practice, many people allow technique to take a back seat to ego by racing from start to finish as quickly as they can. They may ski fast, but only in terms of velocity. In racing, velocity needs to be accompanied by "skiing smart." This means skiing the fastest line, using proper technique, making effective recoveries, and concentrating on the proper course tactics. The guidelines, drills, and exercises in this chapter will help you to fully appreciate skiing smart in a race course and provide you with useful insights and practical advice on how to make recreational racing an important part of your skiing.

Technique and Tactics

Throughout this chapter you will see two terms used often. *Technique* is the way we ski and *tactics* is how technique is applied in a given situation. As you begin to train for recreational racing it will be important to distinguish these terms so you know when you are working on technique and when you are improving tactics. Keep in mind that the two work together. As you improve your technique, you will be able to make tactical changes to improve your race times. This will open the door for more technical improvements, and so on.

A third term is *style*, which refers to the way a person applies technique. Due to size, strength, and body type, all individuals have subtleties to their technique, which comprise their style. If your style does not conform to modern, efficient technique, however, it will inhibit your progress. When watching and copying someone else's skiing, make sure you are observing and mimicking proper technique and not improper individual style.

Alpine Race Events

When you begin recreational racing, the two events you will probably experience are slalom and giant slalom. Coin-op, NASTAR, or league courses may be between slalom and giant slalom. If you progress to the level of USSA amateur racing or Masters racing you can experience super G and downhill racing, but for now concentrate on the specifics of slalom and giant slalom.

In race courses the path to be skied is dictated by a series of gates. Gates are bamboo or plastic poles with colored flags tied to their tops. The color of the flags alternate between red and blue. Each gate has inside and outside poles—the skier has to pass an imaginary line between the poles.

Slalom gates are typically marked by single poles, inside and outside with a small rectangular flag or no flag at all. Giant slalom gates have two poles marking the inside and outside with a large rectangular flag between them (see figure 8.1). Some recreational race courses may be set with only the inside, or turning, pole and no outside pole and flag; the format of other recreational race courses is two side-by-side courses. With dual courses one will be marked with red flags and the other with blue flags. You will ski either the red or the blue course. Often dual courses are used for head-to-head racing.

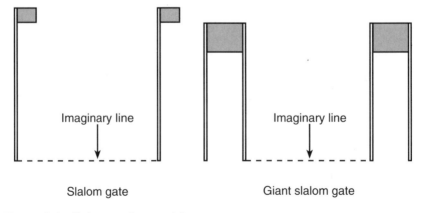

Figure 8.1 Slalom and giant slalom gates.

This format can be fun and great training for you and a buddy, sibling, or son or daughter.

Giant slalom arguably represents natural skiing in speed, turn size, and turn shape. For this reason, most recreational race courses are giant slalom or modified giant slalom. Giant slalom courses have a smooth, even rhythm that flows well with the terrain. Free ski an intermediate trail with medium-radius turns, and you will probably be making typical giant-slalom turns (see figure 8.2).

A slalom course is a test of quickness and agility because it is the course with the most turns in the shortest distance. In slalom, the course is usually a series of rhythmic, quick turns. Slalom courses can have several types of gates. Open gates are set across the hill, while

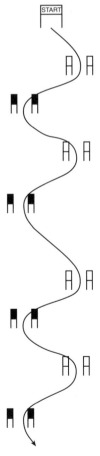

Figure 8.2 Sample section of a giant slalom course.

closed gates are set vertically down the hill. Vertical combinations are made up of two or more closed gates together. These consist of a *hairpin* (two closed gates in a row) and *flushes* (three or more closed gates in a row). See figure 8.3.

The spacing of slalom and giant slalom turns varies such that the same hill would have approximately three times as many slalom gates set as giant slalom gates in the same distance and vertical drop.

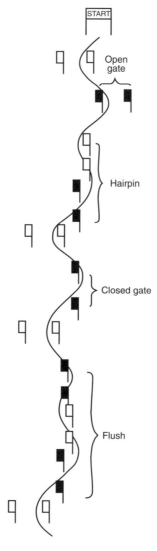

Figure 8.3 Sample section of a slalom course.

Ski racing is a timed event; we are always racing the clock to improve our time. In each turn or series of turns we should strive to find a faster technique or faster line. This will not only improve our ski racing experience, it will also improve our overall skiing level because it will demand more perfection out of everything we do in our skiing. Working hard at ski racing will make you a better skier.

FUNDAMENTAL COMPONENTS OF SKI RACING

It is exciting to watch elite ski racers perform. These ski racers excel because they apply the fundamental components of skiing with athleticism and an understanding of tactics learned through years of training. It will help your high-performance skiing to watch World Cup or Olympic ski racing on television or with video tapes. If you are interested in watching World Cup ski racing, you may purchase one of the annual World Cup Winning Runs videos produced by the United States Ski Coaches Association. To obtain these videos, contact the United States Ski Coaches Association at P.O. Box 100, Park City, UT 84060.

The fundamental components of ski racing are the same as those found in all levels of skiing, and are based on the scientific principles involved in biomechanics, physiology, physics, and equipment technology. An understanding of these components will help you in your pursuit of being a better skier. A knowledgeable racer can be his or her own best coach.

Knowledge of physics is an integral part of understanding alpine ski technique. The relevant force components can be quite complex. However, a basic knowledge is helpful when analyzing technical and tactical elements. The forces influencing skiing can be broken down into internal and external forces.

Internal Forces

Internal forces are forces produced by the muscular effort of the skier. Examples of internal forces are the extension and flexion of the legs and the rotary movements of the feet, legs, hips, and upper body. In efficient skiing it is important to use the forces correctly and in concert with your skeletal support. The world's best ski racers support themselves with their skeletal structure, allowing them to use their muscular structure for maximizing effective, internal forces.

External Forces

External forces are forces existing in nature. Skiers must deal with these forces at all times. How efficiently a skier uses the external forces dictates how efficiently he or she will ski. These are the main external forces found in skiing:

- **Gravitational force** is the vertical pull toward the center of the earth. Components of gravitational force hold skiers to the slope and pull them down the slope. For racers, the fall line, or the path of gravity down the hill, is extremely important. The moments during which our skis are pointed straight down the fall line in each turn are the times of maximum acceleration. Racers continually focus on maximizing acceleration while in the fall line, and maintaining momentum out of the fall line at the end of each turn.

- **Frictional force** is the force between the skis and the snow. We can reduce this force with ski base material, base preparation, and waxes.

- **Drag force** is air resistance.

- **Centrifugal force** is the inertial force that pulls the skier out of the turn. This inertial force acts on the body outward at right angles to the curved path of the skis.

- **Reaction force** is the sum of all the forces acting perpendicular to the ski.

World Cup or Olympic ski racers use internal forces during racing turns to make the best use of gravity. At times racers ski in a low, compact body position, which is more aerodynamic and reduces the drag force. If we studied the bases of racers' skis, we would see that a lot of time had gone into both the base preparation and waxing to reduce the frictional force. The best ski racers in the world continually respond to the various external forces in their skiing environment to reduce the race time on any course.

Center of Mass

When performing high-level skiing or racing, our upper body (torso, head, and arms) often does one thing while the lower body (legs and feet) do another task or movement. This is *upper and lower body separation*. Because all parts are connected, however, we must think about the body as a whole entity.

A person's center of mass is located at the lower stomach or upper hip region in an upright, balanced, athletic stance. The center of mass shifts with every body movement. In angular positions, the exact location of the center of mass will be a point to the inside of the body. The direction of the center of mass is extremely important in racing turns.

HIGH-PERFORMANCE RACING SKILLS

Success in alpine ski racing is based on proper execution of a specific set of skills. *You must master the fundamental skills to master the sport.* In the next sections of this chapter we will detail the fundamental skills of racing and then give you drills and exercises to perfect these skills.

There are four primary technical elements in skiing: balance, rotary movements, edging movements, and pressure control. The latter three elements, working in harmony with balance, are found to some degree in all ski turns (see figure 8.4). The degree of influence

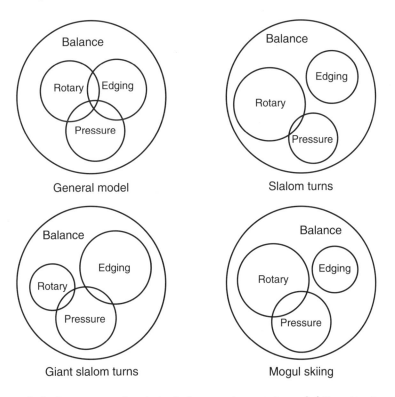

Figure 8.4 Interaction of technical elements in a variety of skiing situations.

of each element depends on snow, slope, turn shape, speed, equipment, and the individual athlete.

Balance

Balance, including the use of a balanced stance, is the most important element in the foundation of all activities on skis. Balancing is the art of maintaining equilibrium, which entails a continuous adjustment of the center of mass in order to compensate for the constant imposition of external forces (see figure 8.5). In skiing, balance is dynamic: equilibrium while in motion. Keep in mind the skills and movements necessary to maintain a desired stance under different conditions of speed, slope, turn size, and surface shape. There are two types of dynamic balance: fore/aft and lateral.

Figure 8.5 Balanced stance for skiing.

When skiing in balance, there is minimal movement needed to change pressure distribution on the skis either fore/aft or laterally. This balanced position allows you to execute movements with minimal muscle contraction without requiring muscle recovery time. When we are out of balance recovery time is required to regain balance. The time required to recover balance increases the time needed to make individual turns, which increases the overall time on a race course. Skiing continually in an out-of-balance position leads to muscle overuse and fatigue.

Maintaining proper fore/aft balance is important in efficient skiing. Three elements of alpine equipment can contribute to balance problems. Skis form a one-and-a-half to two-meter platform base. The binding firmly attaches the boot to the ski. The high, stiff, plastic boot allows us to use the lower leg shaft as a level of support. These factors, while providing many benefits to skiing, allow us to cheat on fore/aft balance. With the ski as a platform, we can move through a wide fore/aft range without falling over. Since the binding firmly attaches our feet to the skis, the same holds true. The stiff ski boot and leg shaft allow a skier to lean against the back of the boot. When we improperly use one or more of these factors, we can maintain an upright stance, but we are not balanced and will not ski efficiently. This is because we are relying on muscular and not skeletal support for our stance.

Lateral, or side-to-side, balance plays an important role throughout the turn. It becomes critical when you turn out of the fall line where the centrifugal force, in addition to the gravitational force, is pulling you out of the turn. You can improve lateral balance by adopting a wider stance.

Drill 1: CENTERED SKIING

On a slope with pitch and terrain that you are comfortable skiing, make a nonstop run of mixed short- and medium-radius turns. Focus on being balanced over the skis throughout each turn and the entire run (see figure 8.6, a and b). If you feel your weight on the balls of your feet and the pressure of your shins against the front of your ski boots, this indicates that your weight is centered over your skis and not too far forward or back. If you feel excessive muscle tension in your legs, alter your stance until the muscles relax. This will assure that you are skiing in a stance supported by your skeletal not muscular structure. Once you have found this centered stance on your skis, progress to more challenging terrain and a wider range of turns feeling the same kinesthetic sensations of the feet, shins, and muscles.

Figure 8.6, a and b
Dynamic balanced skiing.

Drill 2: STRAIGHT RUN

Find a long, nearly flat, uncrowded slope. Go directly down the hill in a straight run. Balance fore and aft over your skis. Stand first on your left ski, picking up the right ski. Then stand on your right ski and pick up the left ski. Find your balanced stance where you can move from one ski to the other without upper body movements while maintaining a perfectly straight direction. This will help you perfect your lateral skiing balance.

Rotary Movements

Rotary movements, which involve a twisting action of the legs or torso, assist in guiding and redirecting the ski in a turn. The predominant rotary movement used in racing turns is *steering*, the muscular guidance of the ski in the turn accomplished by an inward twisting movement of the lower limbs in coordination with edging of the ski. Executed properly, steering will provide muscular guidance to reduce the radius of a turn without excessive skidding of the ski. This lack of skidding is called *carving*.

An additional rotary movement is *pivoting*, which is the twisting of the skis resulting in no change in body direction. Pivoting is used in short turns or in turns where the radius is too tight to allow complete carving of the skis. Pivoting should be minimized in racing turns.

It is extremely difficult to use rotary movements to steer with the legs in a turn if proper balance is not maintained. When working on rotary movement drills, remember to also focus on a balanced stance.

If you watch a video of World Cup slalom and giant slalom skiing, you can see the difference between giant slalom racers steering the skis into a turn and slalom racers pivoting them into a turn. This shows the art of applying the most efficient technical element for each changing situation.

Drill 1: HOCKEY STOP

Start in a straight run to gain a little speed. Then quickly pivot both skis under your body into a sideslip in the fall line. Sideslip to a stop, first to your left side and then to your right. Do the entire drill in a straight line in the fall line. As you pivot your feet be sure to keep your weight centered over your feet and not too far forward or back (see figure 8.7).

Figure 8.7 Hockey stop.

Drill 2: ROTARY WEDGE TURNS

Begin a straight run down an easy slope with the skis in a wedge position. Keeping both skis relatively flat on the snow, change directions by turning your feet first to the left and then to the right (see figure 8.8, a and b). As you get comfortable with these turns, explore changing direction more or less by the amount you steer, or turn, your feet.

Edging

The angle of the ski on the snow (edge angle) is a factor that determines the turn radius. Angulation of the body toward the center of a turn helps control the edge angle. Skis produce the appropriate edge angle through a continual adjustment in the hip, knee, and ankle joints.

A leaning, or tilting, of the entire body is called *inclination* and is another form of angulation. The three types of angulation, hip, knee, and ankle, can be supplemented with inclination of the body toward the center of the turn in order to resist higher external forces. Straight

Figure 8.8, a and b Rotary wedge turns.

body inclination might be powerful in resisting the centrifugal force; however, it is slow due to shifts of total body mass from side to side, and is generally not used in slalom and giant slalom.

Drill I: SIDESLIPS

On a moderate slope, stand in a traverse position facing across the hill. Release the edges of your skis by flattening them. You can do this by moving your knees down the fall line. As you release your edges, the skis will slide sideways down the hill. To slow down or stop, move your knees inward, toward the hill, to increase edge angle. Do the drill facing both ways so that both your left and right skis get a chance to be the downhill ski (see figure 8.9).

Figure 8.9 Sideslipping.

Drill 2: DYNAMIC WEDGE TURNS

Choose a slope a little steeper than the slope you used for the Rotary Wedge Turns. Go straight down the hill in a wedge position (see

Figure 8.10, a and b Dynamic wedge turns with edging.

figure 8.10, a and b). While maintaining the wedge position, transfer most of your weight to the left ski. Increase the edge angle of that ski by tipping the left knee inward. You will turn to the right. Then transfer most of your weight to the right ski and tip the right knee inward. You will turn to the left. The turns will become easier if you flatten the ski that is on the inside of the turn at the same time that you increase the edge angle on the outside ski.

Pressure Control

The sidecut and construction of a modern race ski allow it to turn if you apply the right elements. If you put your ski on edge and apply pressure in a balanced stance, the ski will turn an arc on the snow. The pressure on the skis results from a combination of gravity (weight), centrifugal force, and changes in terrain. The pressure that the skis exert on the snow is not evenly distributed along the skis nor does it remain constant throughout the turn. Controlling pressure is the action of adjusting the pressure exerted by the skis on the snow throughout the turn. This includes flexion and extension movements, edging, and weight distribution.

Drill 1: FALLING LEAF

Begin with the sideslip that we did in the edging drills. As the skis are sliding down the fall line, move your weight forward by either pressing against the front of the boots or by leaning forward. This will cause the skis to sideslip forward across the hill. Move your weight back by standing on the heels of your feet or by leaning back. The sideslip will now be in a backward direction to the fall line. Do the drill facing in both directions. This drill will demonstrate the effects of fore/aft pressure.

Drill 2: OUTSIDE SKI TURNS

On a slope of moderate terrain, make medium-radius turns with all of your weight on the outside ski in each turn. This will commit the maximum amount of pressure to the outside (turning) ski (see figure 8.11). You will discover better turn mechanics by the increased pressure and also better lateral balance over the outside ski. As you become comfortable with these turns, progress to more difficult terrain and varying turn sizes.

Figure 8.11 Outside ski turns.

The elements of rotary movements, edging movements, and pressure control, when in concert with a balanced stance and directed by center of mass movements, form the basic foundation for good racing turns. These elements must not be in conflict with each other. You must be able to maintain balance throughout the turn before you can effectively carry out detailed work on rotary movements, edging movements, and pressure control. In the remaining parts of this chapter we will provide you with drills and exercises to perfect these primary technical elements.

APPLICATION OF ALPINE TECHNIQUE

Every turn is a unique blend of the different physical components and technical elements. This blend is based on adaptation and feedback control. In racing, our turn shape and radius are dictated by gate placement. This also means that for any turn, or group of turns, there is optimum acceleration to generate and momentum to maintain. How efficiently we blend the technical elements with the physical components in each turn will translate into how fast we ski the course. This is the application of alpine technique.

This is a good time to go back to chapter 2 and review how ski geometry and construction, edge angle, and pressure distribution can create carved turns. These are critical now because efficiency translates directly into time on the clock.

Body positions play a key role in the execution of dynamic turns. The upper and lower body must work in harmony and their relationship must be managed throughout the turn in order to stay in balance and effectively create, transmit, and resist forces. Your stance should always be dynamic and not static. Using your upper and lower body correctly will allow you to create the proper angles with your skeletal and muscular structure and facilitate effective use of the ski design.

Shawn Smith, long-time coach of the Professional Ski Instructors of America's Demonstration Team, describes dynamic movement throughout the turn as "balancing into the future." Aldo Radamus, former United States Ski Team (USST) Head Men's Technical Coach, says that a skier not actively moving throughout the turn, but skiing in a static, fixed position, will always be slow.

Angulation

Angulation of the body enables the ski to be edged on the snow. The required amounts of edge angle vary considerably depending on the slope you are skiing and your desired direction change. On steep terrain, and with round turns, the major angulation will be obtained through the hip assisted by the knee and ankle joints. On flatter terrain, because the forces are not so great, you need less edge angle, and can create it with knee and ankle angulation and possibly subtle hip angulation.

In racing turns always strive for efficiency. Use only the appropriate amount of angulation to overcome the external forces. Over-angulation on flatter terrain results in overedging and slows the skier. Not enough angulation, and thereby insufficient edge angle, on steeper terrain results in skidding. A skidding ski does not travel as fast as a carving ski and so the skier will lose speed.

Ten Tips to Tune Up Your Racing

Every good skier who races and every good racer who free skis knows that one complements the other. Most certainly, serious skiers who race benefit from blending their free-skiing skills into more course-restricted racing skills. It's important that you understand just how this can work for your racing. To this end, here are some tips on recognizing the connection between free skiing and racing, while focusing on skiing techniques specific to racing.

Tip 1: When you first get into racing, if possible ski only recreational giant slalom courses. These courses are generally set to have rhythmical and rounder-shaped turns. This is just the kind of turning environment you want when getting started in racing.

Tip 2: Your line through the gates is critical. Skiers may have different lines depending on how early or how late they initiate their turns and the degree of carving they have. It's important that you find the line that is most efficient for your type of skiing.

Tip 3: As you progress in your racing on more advanced courses, it's important to look at least two to three gates ahead so you are prepared to change your turning rhythm to adjust to changes in the gate pattern. While free skiing, you can challenge your ability to turn on demand by picking out bumps, trees, or other objects and planning to finish your turn when you get to them, as if they were gates laid out on the course.

Tip 4: You've got to be able to carve your skis while free skiing if you expect to carve them while racing.

Tip 5: Your hip is the focus in a good racing curve in giant slalom. You've got to keep your hip to the inside of the turn. The hip angulation that's created prevents skidding and maintains the carving of your outside ski.

Tip 6: Don't pinch the gate; that is, don't get your feet too close to the gate while turning. This actually causes you to skid and lose your line. Instead, get your hip near the gate with your feet two or more feet away from the gate, maintaining your carving.

Tip 7: Come up out of a turn in a forward direction down the hill to keep your center of mass with the center of your skis. If you let the skis get ahead of you, you have to spend too much time correcting your balance, and in so doing you can lose not only time but your line as well.

Tip 8: Your hands need to be in front of your body. Think of the tips of your skis and your hands as the first objects to pass the gate and you'll keep your weight forward.

→

Tip 9: You've got to be aware of your shoulders. When your shoulders are not square with the hill, you may lean into the hill, which causes your skis to skid, and again you lose your carve and your line. If the hands are forward, your downhill hand should be lower in order to influence your shoulders to tip square with the hill, also influencing your hip to angulate to help maintain your carve. So, with a right turn, the left arm is lower.

Tip 10: You can make or break a race depending on your start and finish. To gain a timing advantage at the start, project your chest and upper body down the hill, pushing off with your poles to propel your body down the starting ramp and into the race course. In this way, your feet enter the course last, hitting the wand that starts the timing clock after your upper body is already into the race. For the finish make your last turn straight—that is, on most race courses the last gate is set to ski straight through it. So for the last two gates, pick the straightest line and try to get to the finish without arching any turns.

Here are a few more notes:

• You need to find your "100 percent" when racing, and it may actually mean skiing less aggressively than you think. Your 100 percent through the course is the fastest speed you should ski through the course given your racing ability, skiing style, the type of course, and so on, not necessarily the fastest you can ski down the hill were the course not there. Measured against your absolute speed, your 100 percent race course speed may be only 80 percent of your all out speed.

• Use the race hill to your advantage. If you are a steep slope skier, ski the steepest part of the course aggressively. Similarly, if you are a good flats skier and glide well, you should take advantage of the flat part of the course. Also use the snow conditions. If it's a bit slushy, there's new-fallen snow, or it's icy, think about how you currently ski these conditions, and take this knowledge with you into the course.

• Generally, when learning to race it's best to race within yourself, and against yourself. This helps you to focus on skiing the course rather than skiing against another skier on a course parallel to yours, or against the skier that just went before you. An advantage that coin-operated courses offer is the opportunity to do a run, experiment with technique, and then go back up and try it again using the same or another strategy. In this way, the course becomes a training partner, but it shouldn't be your only partner because it won't observe how you ski the course!

—Brent Boblitt

Angulation Tips

1. Use ankles, knees, and hips to create edging.
2. Use only the amount of angulation necessary, as determined by speed, steepness, turn size, and snow surface.
3. It is important that hip angulation does not adversely affect fore/aft balance. You will be in a position where the hip moves inside the feet. However, if the hips move further back than the feet, then you will lose fore/aft balance.

Pressure Distribution

You can perform a carved turn by tipping the ski on edge and then applying pressure to the edge. Where the pressure is applied is critical to the ski's performance. Due to sidecut and ski design, pressure needs to be applied to the forebody of the ski at the top or beginning of the turn. Balance over the balls of the feet and apply pressure to the front of the boots. This will put pressure on the inside front edge of the skis, allowing them to carve into the turn (see figure 8.12).

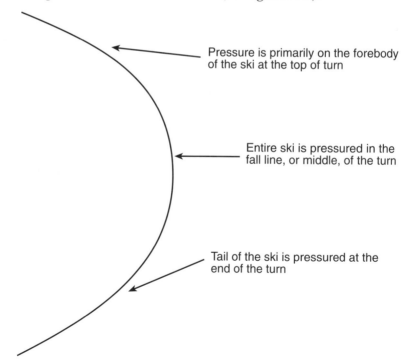

Pressure is primarily on the forebody of the ski at the top of turn

Entire ski is pressured in the fall line, or middle, of the turn

Tail of the ski is pressured at the end of the turn

Figure 8.12 Pressure distribution throughout a turn.

It is important to have pressure over the entire length of the ski as it comes into the fall line in the middle of the turn. This way, the entire ski can be bending, which will use all of the sidecut and allow for optimal turning of the skis. The pressure, which comes primarily from body weight, should be focused on the outside ski.

The external forces working against you will be the greatest from the exit of the fall line until the finish of the turn. Centrifugal force pushes you out of the turn and gravity pushes you down the hill, or out of the turn. You need to distribute the pressure along the entire ski. The forces also tend to push you back on the skis, so counter this by keeping the hips over the ski boots.

Pressure Distribution Tips

1. Always start a turn by pressuring the front of the skis.
2. Keep pressure against the fronts or tongues of the boots.
3. Keep both skis on the snow, but most of your weight on the outside ski.
4. In the last half of the turn you should be standing on the center of the ski with the entire ski pressured.
5. Resist the forces that push you onto the tails of the skis at the end of the turn by keeping pressure against the fronts of the boots.

Upper Body and Lower Body Separation

In high-performance skiing it is important to separate movements of the upper body (torso, arms, and head) from movements of the lower body (hips, legs, and feet). In linked ski turns, keep the upper body quiet, and use only needed, efficient movements. The arms are 10 percent of total body weight—inappropriate use will adversely affect performance. Arms should be held forward of the body comfortably, and never out of your range of view. This position will help with good fore/aft balance. Skiing in a stance with the shoulders level to the slope will help you maintain a balanced stance. In slalom, you may use your arms to clear the gate pole. Do this without moving the arms.

Keeping your feet hip-width apart will facilitate independent legwork and give you better lateral balance. Both skis should stay on the snow throughout the turn, but the outside ski is dominant.

Upper and Lower Body Tips

1. Arms forward and quiet.
2. Level shoulders.
3. Feet hip-width apart.

RACING TACTICS

The tactics you use in high-performance recreational racing relate to the proper application of technique in given race situations. Good technique is the focus of a ski-racing turn, with the gate dictating the exact size and shape of the turn. The gates above and below indicate exactly where to begin and end the turn. Two other tactical points are skiing the proper line and timing the turn properly.

Timing and Line

The line is the path you need to take in order to make the best turns and, therefore, to be fast. For any combination of turns, there is an optimal time to start and finish each turn. A good line, with proper timing of movements, will take you smoothly and speedily from gate to gate throughout the length of the course.

The two types of turns in slalom and giant slalom recreational ski racing depend on where the gates are set. When gates are set across the fall line a considerable change of direction is required for each turn, and the turns are rounded, or more complete. Therefore, the correct line is one where most of the turn, as much as 65 to 75 percent, is made above the gate (see figure 8.13). As one turn is finished, the skis and body are directed such that the turn can be made above the next gate. If both the inside and outside poles of the gate are set, a good visual key is to aim at the outer third of the gate. This will give the height and direction for a technically correct turn.

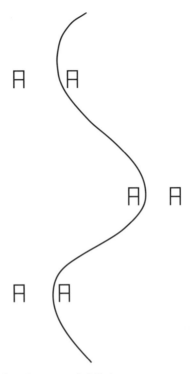

Figure 8.13 Proper line for out-of-fall-line turns.

If the terrain is flatter and the gates are set more in the fall line, there will be a minimal amount of direction change in each turn. Half of the turn can be completed at the gate with the other half completed below the gate (see figure 8.14). In this type of turn, finish a turn with the skis and body aimed at the inner third of the next gate. This will allow you to ski the proper line, without overturning and adding time to the course.

For each gate, imagine a line that runs through the turning pole both above and below the pole. This line, called the *rise line*, is on the fall line of the turning pole. Start each turn as you cross the rise line of the gate and and finish each turn as you cross the rise line below the gate (see figure 8.15).

Proper tactics are a combination of skiing the correct line and timing the start and finish of each turn in order to make high quality technical turns. A common mistake of many inexperienced racers is focusing on the turning pole and turning at the pole. Look at the figures for timing and line to see how the turn is shaped around the

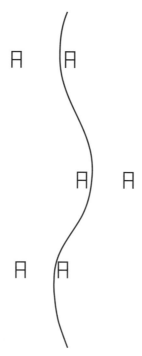

Figure 8.14 Proper line for fall-line turns.

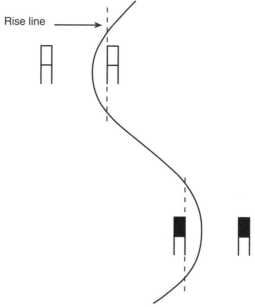

Figure 8.15 Rise line and path of skier.

gate. This will help you visualize where and in what direction you want to finish the turn. With a little practice, you will develop the touch to start the turn on the correct line and at the proper time.

When you first start skiing courses, focus on timing and line, and do not worry about your race times. Later, make small adjustments in both of these and see how the adjustments relate to time: if you are faster, you know that the adjustment is beneficial. Over time you will develop a sense of when and where to ski both slalom and giant slalom courses.

Rhythm Changes

Rarely is a race course made up of only one type of turn. Due to changes in the slope or changes made by the course setter, courses often switch from one type of turn to the other. So, once you have learned how to ski both fall-line and out-of-the-fall-line turns, your next step will be practicing changing line from one type of turn to the other. *Rhythm change* is going from fall-line to out-of-fall-line turns, or vice versa. The line adjustment to these changes is best made one gate above the actual rhythm change. The key to rhythm changes is to look ahead. How and where you finish a turn depends on the next two turns that are approaching. It is important to look two or three gates ahead to ski the best line.

Terrain Changes

Changes in race course terrain for which you need to be prepared are changes from steeps to flats, changes from flats to steeps, and small changes. You will have to deal with these terrain changes on every race course you ski.

When confronting small terrain changes in a race course maintain a balanced stance and maintain contact between your skis and the snow. As you approach a small terrain change, press forward against the fronts of your boots. This will keep your weight moving forward and you will maintain your balance. You may also extend or retract your legs, like shock absorbers, to keep your skis pressured on the snow.

When a race course goes from flat to steep or steep to flat, it is important to adjust your line in order to optimize your performance. Follow two simple guidelines. First, when you ski from a steep course onto flatter terrain, run the last two gates of the steeps on a straighter line than you normally would. This will let you carry more speed from the steeps onto the flats and you will be faster overall.

You have the opportunity to gain speed in the steeps, while you should try to maintain your momentum on the flats.

Second, if you are skiing from the flat onto the steep part of a course, make a round turn in the last gate before the steep (the gates on the flats tend to be in the fall line). This way you will set yourself up to ski the turns on the steep on the correct line. Racers often make the mistake of going too straight right onto the steep, and then they must struggle on a low, slow line through a series of gates. Setting up for the last gate of the flat will sacrifice little speed and you will quickly benefit from the correct line on the steep.

Tips on Tactics

1. Round, or out-of-the-fall-line turns, should be 65 to 75 percent finished above the gate (at the turning pole).
2. Straight, or in-the-fall-line turns, need only 50 to 60 percent of the turn made at the turning pole.
3. Always look two to three gates ahead.
4. In rhythm changes, straighten out the last round gate when going from round to fall-line turns.
5. In rhythm changes, ski a round line in the last fall-line gates in a section that goes from fall-line to round turns.

MENTAL PREPARATION

Well-known coach and sport psychologist Jack Donohue likes to say, "It's not just a question of getting rid of butterflies. It's a question of getting them to fly in formation." Donahue's quote sums up mental preparation. Getting the butterflies to fly in formation is a mental directive you give yourself. Use the churning emotions and sensations you feel in your gut to invigorate your muscles and limbs so that you can achieve maximum performance.

In high-performance skiing, whether recreational racing or another area, once you gain control of your thinking, you can control the butterflies. Concentration, arousal, visual imagery, goal-setting, and self-confidence will allow you to perform at accelerated levels.

Concentration

Concentration is the ability to focus your attention. Keven Burnett, Executive Director of the Mount Bachelor Ski Education Foundation and a former U.S. Ski Team Downhill Coach writes about concentration in *Personal Training Organizer for Alpine Skiing*: "What you focus on is what your brain sees either consciously or subconsciously. It can be thought of as your mind's camera that must be actively focused to get the best results. For a successful performance you must be able to focus on specific cues in the competitive environment, and ignore any distractions that might exist."

There are specific, positive cues you can use in your skiing to focus your mind's camera, for instance, "look ahead," "stand on the outside ski," "hands forward," or "pressure against the fronts of the boots." You will come up with cues that relate to your skiing and make sense in focusing your mind. These cues help keep distractions or negative thoughts out of your mind.

Arousal

Keven discusses arousal as follows: "Arousal is essentially the amount of physical and mental energy that you have running through your body in a given situation. Arousal can be thought of as your body's engine speed. When you are relaxed your arousal is low. When you are extremely worried your arousal is high. To perform at your best you need to have just the right amount of arousal. Too little or too much arousal will hurt your performance. You must identify the specific level of arousal that you need for your optimal performance state."

Keven gives two suggestions for reaching your optimal performance state. "To relax use patterned breathing. Patterned breathing is simply slowing down your breathing rate to half its normal rate (once every five to ten seconds). Breathing properly requires you to inhale through your nose and exhale through your mouth. With each exhale, feel the tension leave your body. Close your eyes and feel your neck and shoulders unwind and relax. As you relax you will feel your shoulders drop slightly and you will feel more grounded. Continue this breathing until your muscles feel loose and your thoughts clear. Practice for five minutes daily and in a variety of situations."

"To increase your arousal level you can either use music or physical activity as the preferred methods. Simply listening to music can get you highly charged. Put together a tape that has songs that get your feet moving. Have this tape with you in your walkman to use when you need to get charged up. If you don't have music available, then simply do some high energy activity. This will get your blood flowing and will boost your energy."

Visual Imagery

With imagery training we create pictures in our minds of how to do something. However, it takes practice to incorporate this imagery into our athletic performances. The more specific the visual image one produces, the more vivid the image will be.

Many studies have proven the success of visual imagery. A classic study involved basketball players shooting free throws. At the start of the study individuals in each of three groups practiced and then recorded their success in making free throws. Subsequently, group one shot free throws only. Group two spent some time shooting free throws and some time visualizing the shooting of free throws. Group three never shot any free throws; they only visualized the movements. At the end of the study the individuals were tested again on their success with free throws. Group two, with both practicing and imaging, had the greatest percentage increase in successful free throws. The group who had only visualized showed more improvement than the group who had only shot free throws. Visual imagery works and it can work for you in high-performance skiing.

When creating images use as many of the five senses as possible. For example, feel the cold wind on your face; see the course or terrain coming at you; hear the gate panels go by as you make each turn; and feel your skis carving smoothly through the snow. In order for the images to be helpful, they must be images of skills and movements you are capable of performing. It will do no good to try and visualize Alberto Tomba skiing slalom if you are a beginning parallel skier.

Videotaping can help you create your visual images. Have someone videotape you skiing your best, and then use the video as the basis for your imaging. Beginning ski racers often make better turns when free skiing than when skiing in courses. Watch a video of yourself free skiing in slalom or giant slalom turns, use that as your skiing image, and mentally superimpose the turns onto a race course. In this way you can visualize skiing that you are fully capable of performing. A visual image becomes the first step in mental rehearsal for an event, for a training session, or when thinking about skiing in the off-season.

Goal-Setting

When you start getting involved in recreational racing and decide that it is something you want to pursue, it is time to think about establishing goals. Most racers realize that goal-setting is an important tool to direct training and racing progress, to stay motivated and focused, and to cope with stress.

Write down your ski-racing goals at least once a year. This will provide initial guidance and direction for training and performance. Come back often to review your goals. Even if you are not serious about racing, goal-setting will benefit all areas of high-performance skiing.

Goals should be short-term, intermediate, and long-term. Long-term and intermediate goals are usually set at the beginning of the year, while short-term goals can be adjusted weekly or daily. Long-term goals may be the overall goal of the season (for example, to win the club championships) or may be multi-year in length. Spend a minimal amount of time thinking about long-term goals. Intermediate goals should focus on a specific part of a season: getting in preseason shape in the fall, working on a particular technical problem over a one-month period, or accomplishments to be made on a one-week trip. Intermediate goals help keep thoughts in perspective, but need not focus on daily progress.

Short-term goals deal with specific training programs and their component parts. Short-term goals can enhance work on a specific problem or skill. Examples of short-term goals include learning a specific technical skill, memorizing a long race course, and eliminating an error in your skiing. Establishing a short-term goal before running a race course can be an excellent way to focus and improve.

The goals that you set should be challenging and yet reasonable enough to direct and motivate you to improvement and eventually excellence. Goals must be attainable. Lastly, goals need to be measurable so you can identify when they have been attained.

Self-Confidence

Keven Burnett has spent the last 10 years working with elite athletes, including the medal-winning U.S. Ski Team during the 1994 Winter Olympic Games in Norway. He says, "One of the most common traits found in elite level athletes is their high degree of self-confidence. Success and self-confidence are interrelated. What you think about can have an effect on your performance. Your optimal performance state needs to reflect a high degree of self-confidence and positive self-talk. Successful athletes think they 'can' and usually 'do.' Unsuccessful athletes 'don't' think they can, and usually 'don't.' It is very important to develop a positive mind-set to experience success. If you are not confident in your ability and you continually tell yourself this, you become more prone to lower the effort that you exert for a performance."

Positive self-talk helps self-confidence. Many of us got our first lesson in positive self-talk at about age five when a parent or teacher read us the book *The Little Engine That Could*. When we make negative statements to ourselves, we undermine our self-confidence. We need to replace the negative statements with positive ones. Develop the habit of addressing situations positively, not negatively. For example, "I can ski this course by skiing a high line," or "I can eat up the crud snow in this bowl," or "Staying balanced in these moguls will make this run a piece of cake."

Visualization, arousal regulation, and goal-setting have a positive effect on your self-confidence because they make you focused and prepared. Then you have the mental state of a successful high-performance skier.

COURSE INSPECTION

The art of inspecting a course is another aspect of ski racing for you to master. When racing on NASTAR or coin-operated courses inspection is not important because the courses tend to be simple and straightforward on smooth, consistent terrain. However, as you look for more challenges, you will experience longer, more demanding courses. In order to maximize your performance it is in your best interest to learn how to inspect and study a course.

There are many variables in race courses due to snow conditions, weather, snow surface, and alterations in terrain. Also, course setters each have their own style. Thus, race courses on the same hill differ from day to day and race to race. In many instances you will only get one or two runs on a course.

For these reasons, study the course before you race it. Look at the snow surface conditions, gate placement, any tough or tricky places, and any easy sections. Then you can maximize your performance when you ski the course. Here are some guidelines for course inspection:

1. Know the rules for course inspection. The rules change from area to area and depending on the level of competition.
2. Start early so you have plenty of time. It is good to inspect the course and then have time to ski and warm up before your start.

3. Do not try to memorize the entire course. Until you have more experience, it will probably confuse you.

4. Determine the three or four most critical parts of the course. These may be difficult terrain sections, hard gate placements, or changes in snow conditions. Make a plan for how you want to ski each of these sections. Pick some kind of landmark or indicator so you will know when you are approaching these sections.

5. Identify places where you have to make special line decisions, such as where you need to set up before a steep pitch, where you can ski straight and gain a little more speed onto a flat section, or where you need to set up for a difficult combination of turns. Make a plan for each of these.

6. Check the snow surface conditions to be sure your skis are properly prepared.

7. At each of the sections you have studied and planned for, take a moment to stop, close your eyes, and visualize the section and how you will ski it.

8. On the lift on the way back up the mountain, close your eyes and visualize each of these sections again. Do this at least one more time, at the start before your run.

9. If you are running later in the race, watch the first few skiers in some of the more critical sections. This will help in your mental preparation.

KEYS TO HIGH PERFORMANCE

1. Recreational ski racing can be a fun and exciting high-performance challenge for an athletic, intermediate skier.

2. Most ski resorts offer some type of training and racing for the recreational ski racers. The training and racing will center around slalom and giant slalom.

3. To improve your high-performance ski racing, understand how the primary technical elements of balance, rotary movements, edging movements, and pressure control are involved in all ski turns.

4. Maintaining good dynamic balance, supported by your skeletal structure, is the most important element of high-performance skiing.

5. In efficient, high-performance ski-racing turns, the skis are steered onto an edge and then pressure is applied to facilitate turning.

6. The key components of tactics in alpine ski racing are the timing of the turn and the line to be skied; both relate to the gate to be skied around.

7. Practice concentration and focus to improve efficiency in ski racing.

8. You must learn to control your arousal level in order to reach your optimal performance state for competition.

9. Practicing visual imagery can have a positive effect on competing.

10. Setting short-, medium-, and long-term goals provides motivation and performance markers for progress in ski racing.

11. Self-confidence breeds success.

CHAPTER 9

FINE-TUNING YOUR HIGH-PERFORMANCE SKILLS

One of the frustrating aspects of skiing is becoming stymied, and thereby inhibited, by our inabilities on skis. We wish we could carve a turn with minimal skidding; get by a certain knoll in a race course; feel relaxed while skiing moguls; execute a rhythmic pole-touch for an entire mile-long run; stop on a dime; ski for long distances without becoming fatigued; and smoothly link turn after turn in a variety of conditions.

Almost all skiers have technical deficiencies in their skiing. While these errors or lack of skills may not keep you from skiing the runs and conditions you like, you will not ski them with the efficiency and effectiveness desired. Flaws in skills keep you from skiing the moguls, powder, or steeps as relaxedly and smoothly as you would like; cause apprehension at higher speeds or difficult conditions; force you into expending too much energy; or, make you three or four seconds slow on the race course.

It is important to recognize the problems and skill errors and challenge yourself to correct them. In this chapter we will identify some skill problems and provide drills and exercises to correct them or to develop better skills. We will also explain how to best use ski school lessons to improve your skiing.

COMMON PROBLEM AREAS

Georg Capaul, coach of the U.S. Women's "B" and "C" Ski Teams, is candid about what he sees on the slopes. "Most recreational skiers," he says, "have real technical problems and need a lot of work on basic fundamentals." His fundamentals include

- being balanced on your skis, both fore/aft and laterally;
- being able to respond to all conditions with a proper pole-plant, an upright stance on skis, and even weight distribution along the entire length of the outside ski while turning;
- skiing square to the fall line; and
- keeping your head up and looking ahead (what Georg calls "high beam" skiing).

You need to master these basics, Georg says, before you are ready to deal with advanced technical skills. "A problem modern recreational skiers have is that due to all the grooming, it's easy to go fast, and many equate going fast with intermediate skiing. Unfortunately, when the fundamentals are lacking, going fast is not intermediate skiing. Still, these skiers go out on groomed trails and say, 'Yeah, I can handle this,' but were these skiers skiing at a time when trails were skier-packed, rough and mogully, they might be very beginning skiers. In a way, the groomed trails have hurt ski schools because before, skiers needed instruction to get down steep hills; today, they feel they can handle anything . . . that's groomed. Ski schools teach basic fundamentals, and lessons are an essential part of high-performance skiing."

The drills and exercises in this chapter address the key problem areas common among recreational skiers:

- Over-rotating the upper body while turning
- Lack of carving (excessive skidding) while turning
- Lack of rhythmic pole use
- Overall lack of extension/movement in skiing; lack of edge control

- Lack of speed control (unfinished turns)
- Lack of variety in turning skills and choice of turn radius
- Tense and static skiing
- Inability to adapt to changing terrain, pitch, and snow conditions

Each problem area is discussed briefly, followed by an explanation of applicable drills and exercises. Some drills and exercises are useful for more than one problem. Sometimes the multipurpose drills and exercises are presented with adaptations according to the particular problem. Other drills and exercises are designed to accomplish more than has been indicated in this chapter; these are presented only for their specific application to the problem under discussion.

A PERSPECTIVE ON DRILLS AND EXERCISES

The drills are narrowly focused opportunities to learn by doing. They are not a critique of your skiing. They are sensory as well as mechanical experiences. The exercises are broadly focused opportunities to draw your skills together while concentrating on the task of the exercise. In order to profit from technical skill drills, it is important to understand the technical foundation of skiing you learned in earlier chapters.

When doing drills and exercises, be amenable to the changes that will creep into your skiing. Use precision; the purpose of the drills and exercises is not to make you change but to expose your body to a host of biomechanical movements that will let your body make natural adjustments and adaptations to find the perfect rhythm for your style of skiing. Training your body for new muscle memory takes time and repetition. Do drills correctly and repeatedly. Remember, practice does not make perfect—perfect practice makes perfect!

Some drills and exercises will seem complicated and impossible, whereas others may strike you as infantile. These are not reasons to avoid them. The more effort you put into doing a drill as prescribed, the greater the technical benefit to your skiing. You should get to the point where you can perform the drills effortlessly as a warm-up before more aggressive skiing.

You may be thinking about the embarrassment you'll experience while falling all over the mountain trying to do a basic or advanced drill and about how silly you'll look performing drills on beginner slopes when you consider yourself an advanced skier. These egotistic thoughts get in the way of high-performance skiing. The drills are necessary for you to become a better skier.

All members of the U.S. Ski Team spend time every summer practicing skill-enhancing drills. They go back to the basics. Some of these drills will address a particular technical problem or error in their skiing; others may expand or enhance a currently used skill; and other drills may be to learn a new skill or movement. In fact, the U.S. Ski Team has developed a comprehensive battery of skiing skill tests called the USST Basic Alpine Skills Evaluation (USST B.A.S.E.), which is used to improve skiing skill competency at all levels of alpine athlete development in the United States.

Pete Patterson, a former U.S. Ski Team member and medalist in the downhill, believes in practicing the basics to develop high-performance skills. "Learning to ski by picking up the ability to negotiate different terrain in a year's time shows a skier is working real hard on his or her skiing. But, even though this skier appears to be rapidly progressing, you can see the real inexperience in the more subtle aspects of their skiing. It takes years of experience to be able to ski efficiently."

Commenting on the plight of many weekend-only skiers, Pete adds, "Unfortunately, they don't have the opportunity to ski as much as they might like, and they may find it difficult to get to the level at which they feel good. They must be patient, though, because there's just no other way to develop high-performance skills without practice and time.

"What you've got to realize is you always need practice, coaching, or instruction. The best skiers in the world go out, work with a coach, and discover things about their skiing that they're not doing as well as they were a couple of weeks earlier. The coach lets them know; it's really a never-ending process even at the World Cup level. You can always use, and probably forever need, the fine-tuning of a coach, instructor, whomever."

Six Easy Rules for Drills and Exercises

1. Understand what the drill or exercise is designed to accomplish.

2. Be aware of which condition is most appropriate to the drill or exercise, for example, groomed slope, slight bumps, firm snow, soft

snow, bumpy, or steep. Also, know the slope rating for the intended drill or exercise. This rating is adapted from the U.S. Ski Team B.A.S.E. and The National Ski Area Association's trail rating system.

3. Know how to perform the drill. If you perform it incorrectly you may enhance errors and do more harm than good. Further, you won't get the kinesthetic appreciation of your accomplishments: a ski feeling that can accelerate refinement in your skiing when you use it to guide your increasingly more subtle adjustments for skiing in the high-performance mode. If you know what it feels like to hold an edge or angle your hip into the turn, you can replicate this kinesthetic knowledge at certain times during your skiing when you must subtly adjust to get more hip into the hill, more completely finish a turn in the bumps or steeps, or ride your turning ski a little longer in the recreational race course.

4. Commit yourself to a block of skiing time and, unless you're already familiar with the drill or exercise, do it several times to work out the bugs before using an entire run for it. Some drills are frustrating and require lots of practice, especially single-ski skiing, turning and hopping, and angulation. Try these drills each time out until you learn them.

5. Don't avoid difficult or embarrassing drills that cause you to fall down. By doing so, you're likely to ignore aspects of your skiing that are undeveloped. Learning difficult drills will boost your confidence and enhance your skills acquisition.

6. Come back to each drill often. Repetition of proper movements trains muscle memory and automatizes a skill or movement. Only by practicing a new movement often and correctly will it become ingrained into your skiing.

If you can, rehearse some drills at home by thinking through their mechanics and physically arranging yourself (without skis) in the positions called for.

GETTING STARTED
WITH DRILLS AND EXERCISES

In the following section, unless otherwise noted, conditions for the drills are smooth, groomed, firm snow. Where needed, we include explanations of slope and terrain to be used. While it is difficult to describe slopes and terrain consistently throughout the United States, we use the following general terms:

- Beginner: marked green trails, ski school beginner areas, nearly flat.
- Intermediate: marked blue trails, with some pitch to the hill but speed can be controlled.
- Moderate: marked blue trails, similar to intermediate but with an increased pitch that allows for more speed.
- Advanced: marked black trails, with changing terrain.

The environment created by the conditions and slope rating is ideal for doing drills. As a rule, when you can perform drills efficiently, take them to more challenging terrain and variable conditions.

Unless otherwise noted, be in an athletic, skiing stance when performing the drills: skis parallel, hip-width apart; knees slightly bent; hips centered over your skis; upper body relaxed, head up, chest tall; hands and arms forward and always in field of vision; upper back slightly rounded.

The following terms appear throughout the drills and exercises:

- Flex: press down and forward.
- Flex the legs: press the ankles and knees forward.
- Rotate: twist.
- Counter-rotate: move your lower body (legs, boots, and skis) one way, while twisting your upper body (arms, shoulders, head, chest, and upper abdomen) the other, at least as far as facing down the fall line.
- Touch a pole: tap a pole in the snow.
- Plant a pole: decisively push the tip of the pole into the snow.
- Steer: muscularly guide the ski in the turn by inwardly twisting the lower limbs.
- Angulation: the creation of lateral angles in the body for balance on the ski edge; occurs with the ankle, knee, hip or a combination of the three.
- Center of mass: the abdominal region around your navel, between and above your hips, as differentiated from the center of gravity, which can be outside of mass.
- Weight transfer: the shift of body weight from one ski to the other. Usually, weight transfer occurs from the downhill

(outside, or turning) ski to the uphill (inside) ski in preparation for the next turn.

- Downhill, outside, or turning ski: the ski that is doing most of the edging, has the most pressure applied to it, and is closest to the bottom of the hill.
- Uphill or inside ski: the ski that is doing the least amount of edging, has little pressure applied to it (although it is actively turning), and is closest to the top of the hill.

TECHNICAL IMPROVEMENT DRILLS

These are drills that have been selected to assist you in correcting technical problems or to aid in reaching a higher level of high-performance skiing. Feel free to pick and choose the drills that will help you the most.

Pole-Plant Drills

Pole-plants and pole-plant drills can be used to solve many technical problems. Pole swings help re-center your balance to start a new turn. Pole-touches or pole-plants provide rhythm of linked turns and timing of the start of each turn. Pole-plants can also help with leg extension and flexion.

Drill 1: STRAIGHT RUN WITH POLE-PLANTS

On beginner terrain travel down the hill in a straight run. Carry both arms out in front of you as described in Chapter 8 on balanced stance. Keep both forearms quiet and level with your skis. Swing one pole out to the front with your wrist and plant the pole close to the tips of the skis. Then do this pole-swing and pole-plant with the other wrist. Repeat throughout the straight run (see figure 9.1). Remember to

1. swing with the wrist, not arm,
2. plant pole close to tips of skis,
3. keep arms still and parallel to your skis, and
4. establish a rhythm with the pole-swings and pole-plants.

Figure 9.1 Pole–plants in a straight run.

Drill 2: POLE-PLANT TIMING

Two reasons for pole-plants are to time the beginning of the turn and to help create rhythm between turns. This drill helps with the timing and rhythm. On an intermediate slope, start in a traverse. Extend the legs to create a high body position and plant the downhill pole at the same time. Immediately slide the skis around into a new traverse. Don't worry about the quality of the turns—it is the timing of the pole-plant you are developing. Repeat in the other direction and continue down the hill. Focus first on the pole-plant timing. As you develop a rhythm in your turns, add a little speed and make cleaner, more efficient turns.

Drill 3: POLE-PLANTS IN SHORT-SWING TURNS

Select a trail with intermediate terrain. Start straight down the hill, as in the last exercise, with pole-swings and pole-plants. Now begin to execute quick short-radius turns with a pole-plant to initiate each turn. Be sure to plant the pole at the start of each turn, still swinging the pole with the wrist and not moving the arms. Progress to steeper and changing terrain, being sure that every turn begins with a pole-swing and pole-plant near the tips of the skis (see figure 9.2).

Figure 9.2 Pole–plants in short–swing turns.

Drill 4: POLE-PLANTS IN MEDIUM-RADIUS TURNS

Ski a series of linked medium-radius turns on moderate terrain. Initiate each turn with a pole-swing and pole-touch of the downhill pole, in front of the boots (see figure 9.3). Review the four points of a good pole-swing outlined above in the Straight Run With Pole-Plants drill.

Figure 9.3 Pole-plants in medium-radius turns.

Edging Drills

Edging drills will help you make high-performance carved turns. If you have trouble making good carved turns (if you use excessive skidding in your turns), follow the entire progression outlined below. The drills will also help you to finish your turns, allowing better control of speed while skiing.

Drill 1: TRAVERSE

Travel across the hill with both skis on the uphill edges but with most of the weight on the downhill ski. Make the skis track—do not let them lose edge and slip sideways—by flexing the knees and tipping them slightly into the hill. Practice on progressively steeper slopes. As the slope gets steeper, you will note that you must apply more edge (by tipping the knees more into the hill) for the skis to track across the hill. This will give you a feeling of edge adjustment and edge control (see figure 9.4).

Figure 9.4 Traverse.

Drill 2: TRAVERSE WITH EXTENSION AND FLEXION

Begin with a traverse similar to the last exercise. Flexing at the ankles, knees, and hips, sink down into a low body position and then rise to the original position. Repeat the exercise. Practice this until you are comfortable moving from a high, extended position into a low, flexed position by using the ankle, knee, and hip joints. This drill will help you increase both edge awareness and the development of more dynamic movements in your skiing.

Drill 3: SKATING ON SKIS

Find an area of beginner terrain. Skate across this terrain much as you would on ice skates. Push off with one edged ski, transferring the weight onto the other ski. Then push off with that edged ski, transferring the weight back to the original ski (see figure 9.5). Repeat

Figure 9.5 Skating on skis.

the exercise all the way across the terrain. Notice that you develop the edge angle before you push off the ski.

Drill 4: CAMBER TURNS

Select a wide, uncrowded, beginner slope. Start downhill in a good balanced position with your feet hip-width apart. Roll your skis onto the right edges and stand on the edged skis as they carve an arc into the fall line and then back across the hill. Then roll your skis onto the left edges and carve another arc into the fall line and back across the hill. This drill lets you feel how you make a turn just by pressuring the edged ski (see figure 9.6).

Figure 9.6 Camber turns.

Drill 5: SIDESLIPPING WITH EDGE SETS

Stand in a traverse position facing across the hill on groomed, intermediate terrain. Extend the legs to flatten the skis and begin a sideslip down the fall line. Make a firm edge set by sinking down and moving the knees into the hill, then rise to flatten the skis and begin another sideslip. Repeat this drill with sideslips, edge sets, and sideslips. Focus on feeling the edge set and edge release by use of the ankles and knees (see figure 9.7).

Figure 9.7 Sideslipping with edge sets.

Drill 6: WEDGE, EDGE SETS

On intermediate, groomed terrain, link rhythmical wedge turns using the inside edge of the outside ski in each turn. Focus on a feeling of controlling the edge with the ankle and knee as in the Sideslip with Edge Sets drill (see figure 9.8).

Figure 9.8 Wedge edge sets.

Drill 7: CARVED TURNS

On moderate, groomed terrain make smooth, continuous, carved turns. First, focus on making clean arcs through each turn. Next, focus on linking each turn so that the finish of one turn will become the beginning of the next turn. Feel the flow you develop from turn to turn. Experience a variety of turn sizes while maintaining carved arcs.

If one of your problem areas is speed control, continue carving the turn until you are back into a shallow traverse. You can control speed this way. As you continue this in more difficult terrain, you will find that you can control speed on any terrain by controlling turn shape instead of making skidding turns.

Steering and Rotary Movement Drills

Applying rotary movement skills, especially steering, is important to high-performance skiing in all situations. Learning proper steering with the lower body will help you eliminate over-rotating, or twisting, of the upper body. Rotating of the upper body usually happens because the skier does not have good steering skills.

The development of rotary movements with the lower body will add variety to turns. Expanding our use of rotary movements will help us shape our turns and change turn radius to fit terrain, slope, speed, and snow surface. The ability to change turn size and shape also helps control speed.

Drill 1: HEADLIGHT TURNS

Begin on an intermediate slope. Start in a slight wedge making short- to medium-radius turns. Flex your ankle, knee, and hip joints. Think of your knees as car headlights, leading the way in turns. To initiate a turn move your knees in the direction of the turn. This will help you steer the skis into the new turn. As you gain a feeling for this drill, progress to steeper, more difficult terrain.

Drill 2: STEERING INTO TURNS

Find an intermediate slope with few skiers. Traverse the hill. As you gain some momentum, flatten your skis and steer them into the fall line with your feet and knees, then stop with a hockey stop (see figure 9.9). Repeat this several times on both sides. As you become more comfortable steering the skis into the turn, eliminate the hockey stop and continue steering the skis all the way through the turn until you are back in a traverse. Next, link turns by flattening the skis, steering into the fall line, continuing to steer the skis back into a traverse, and then flattening the skis to start the process again.

Figure 9.9 Steering into turn.

Drill 3: SKI POLE DRILL

Too much rotary movement can be a problem in skiing, especially when it comes from rotary movements of the upper body. This drill eliminates excessive upper body guidance in turns. Find a slope with intermediate terrain. Take your pole straps off, put the poles together grip-to-basket, and hold them in your hands, palms up, as if they were a serving tray. Ski down the hill making short-radius turns in the fall line. Keep the poles quiet, level, and facing directly down the hill (see figure 9.10). This drill develops a quiet upper body that continues to face down the hill while the lower body executes short-radius turns.

Figure 9.10 Ski pole drill.

Pressure Control Drills

Controlling pressure on our skis involves the distribution of our body weight, and managing the external forces in any turn. Skis are designed to work best when our body weight is directed toward the front of the ski at the beginning of the turn, and over the entire length of the ski by the end of the turn. In order to counteract the external forces (see Chapter 8), the body weight is usually concentrated on the outside ski in a turn. The following drills will help develop better pressure control.

Drill 1: FALLING LEAF

Review the Falling Leaf drill in Chapter 8 (page 164) to develop feeling for fore/aft pressure distribution.

Drill 2: BIG TOE TO HEEL DRILL

Make medium-radius turns on intermediate, groomed terrain. Initiate each turn by pressing down with the big toe of the outside foot. This will direct the pressure of your body weight to the inside, forward edge of the outside ski. By the time the skis are exiting the fall line in each turn, shift your weight to your heel in order to shift your weight onto the entire ski. Recenter your weight to initiate the next turn with the pressure on your big toe. Practice these linked turns until you are comfortable shifting your body weight throughout each turn.

Drill 3: JAVELIN TURNS

This drill is done on moderate, groomed terrain. Perform javelin turns by turning on the outside ski with the inside ski lifted and held across the front of the outside ski. The inside ski crosses over the turning, or outside, ski only as the turning ski enters the fall line and then the inside ski remains in the javelin position until the turn is completed (see figure 9.11).

Challenging Your Skiing Skills With Snowboarding

A fair number of skiers have bitterly resisted snowboards on "their" mountain, and yet despite all the complaining and sniping, the sport of snowboarding has far outpaced expectations. Even the final bastion of "skiers-only" mountains out West, Alpine Meadows, fully acknowledged snowboarding as a "mainstream" sport in the 1996-97 season by opening its entire mountain to boarders and skiers alike.

Those of us who go both ways on snow have different reasons for doing so, but for me it depends on the conditions and the kind of snow experience I want. Powder days are now almost always snowboard days for me, while ice, hardpack, fast newly groomed snow, and powder bumps are my favorites for skis (although a morning on fast newly groomed snow on my alpine snowboard is a thrill a minute). Racing, on the other hand, is different in that my choice of skis or board depends on the race course as well as the conditions.

Have you ever tried boarding? How long did you stay out? Did you really want to learn, or did you want to be able to say you tried boarding but it wasn't for you? Those are important questions because I believe alpine snowboarding makes a technically sound and better alpine skier. Certainly there's a risk that you'll never again ski if you convert to snowboarding, but most (not all) of the skiers who make this total conversion are intermediate or low advanced skiers. Total converts are unabashed in their celebration of their new sport—they claim it to be more fun and more versatile in varied snow conditions.

There are three general disciplines of snowboarding: alpine, freestyle, and what is called "all-mountain" or combined. Alpine snowboarding is done primarily on snowboards with a symmetric design that has a sidecut for quicker turning and a tip and tail like skis that help you better carve your turns. Asymmetric snowboards are more radically designed at tip and tail and were originally intended for racing. A number of us still ride asymmetric boards for racing and artistic, even radical, carving during free riding on newly groomed slopes. Pros race mostly on symmetric boards. Alpine boards are generally stiff in flex.

Freestyle boarding is tricks, tricks, tricks, and great powder. Most snowboarders ride freestyle. The boards are wider and have tips and tails that are flared up, sometimes quite significantly. Freestyle boards are generally soft in flex.

The all-mountain style of boarding is on snowboards that are a crossover between freestyle and alpine. These boards have a good sidecut, are not as stiff, have a tip and tail with a bit more lip,

→

and are an enjoyable transition board for skiers who want to regularly ski and snowboard.

Want to crossover to boarding to spice up your experience of the mountain and challenge the dynamic balance skills that are so important to high-performance skiing? Here are a few pointers:

1. *Boots.* I advise high-performance skiers to ride on flex-designed, hard-shelled snowboarding boots designed for snowboards and mounted with hard-plate bindings. These are great for serious alpine riding but can be used for all kinds of boarding. I use hard boots and plate bindings on my alpine and freestyle boards. Hard-plate bindings have no release if you fall, as ski bindings do, but falling is really not like falling on skis—it's actually far more controlled on a snowboard. After you've learned to ride, you rarely fall while alpine riding. I don't recommend soft-shelled, lace-up boots with more rigid liners for those who snowboard as a complement to skiing, although for playtime, freestyle boards with appropriate freestyle bindings are a kick if you already know how to ride.

2. *Board.* Again, alpine boards with plate bindings are the best for serious alpine skiers who want to take it to the edge and enhance their skiing skills.

3. *Special talent.* Balance and flexibility are essential for your boarding to begin to enhance your alpine skiing. Racers particularly benefit from the edging extremes afforded riders on alpine boards, and the subtle mechanics of the rounded, carved turn on a snowboard are complementary to patience and rhythm in skiing.

Learning to commit to turns on snowboards, particularly those on your heel or backside, employs important angulation skills that help you stay centered on your skis while in rugged terrain. Similarly, the speed of the descent and the dependence on the lower body to edge the snowboard while the upper body properly settles itself to distribute your weight are additional refinements offered to the high-performance skier.

For the advanced and expert snowboarder and skier, the crossover between the two sports adds yet another enticement: when you have a great day in one sport, it just seems right that you should be granted a similar experience in the other on your next day out!

Figure 9.11 Javelin turns.

Drill 4: WEDGE HOPS

Begin in a wedge position on intermediate, groomed terrain. Maintain the wedge position throughout this exercise. With all of your weight on your left ski, aggressively hop up, move your body across, and land on your right ski. Immediately hop back onto the left ski. Repeat. As you hop from ski to ski keep your weight centered over the ski, not letting it get too far forward or back (see figure 9.12). This drill will help you develop pressure distribution from ski to ski as well as fore/aft on the skis.

Turning Drills

Variety and versatility in turning make high-performance skiing fun and allow us to adapt to day-to-day snow situations. Skiers who can ski all types of snow conditions, terrain, and slopes will enjoy the sport day in and day out. Versatility is not learned quickly; it is

Figure 9.12 Wedge hops.

developed over a long period of time. Take advantage of opportunities to become more versatile. You can do some of the following drills any time and any place. Others require special situations. All of the drills will help you take advantage of terrain and conditions so that you can enjoy any skiing experience and become a better high-performance skier.

Drill 1: BIG TURNS, LITTLE TURNS

On a moderate slope, ski a specific pattern of turns. Keep repeating the pattern throughout the run. Begin by making three short-radius turns followed by three medium-radius turns, and repeat. Next try two medium-radius turns, four short-radius turns, and then two medium-radius turns. Now make three short-radius turns followed by three long-radius turns. Try five short-, three long-, and five short-radius turns. Devise your own more complicated patterns. Take the pattern drill to more difficult terrain and snow conditions.

Drill 2: FOLLOW THE LEADER

With a partner, take turns following each other. The rule is you have to follow the exact track of the leader while making the same size and shape turns. The leader should use a variety of turn sizes and shapes, as well as speed adjustments. For more advanced skiers, playing follow the leader through moguls, powder, trees, and at higher speeds will enhance skiing versatility.

Drill 3: FIGURE EIGHT CONTEST

There is no better way to improve your skills in powder skiing than by doing figure eights with two people. Find an area with untracked powder. The first skier makes a series of linked, consistent, short-radius turns in the untracked powder. The second skier follows, skiing the same turn size and shape but in the opposite direction. This creates figure eight tracks in the snow. This exercise requires rhythmical, consistent turns by the first skier. The second skier is forced into skiing predetermined turns. This drill is fun and challenging and will give you instant feedback when you look back up the hill at your tracks.

Drill 4: SKIING WITHOUT SEEING

On a day when there is new, loose snow on trails, ski with a partner, following only one or two turns behind. Due to the new snow being kicked up, you will not be able to see your skis, feet, and little terrain changes. You will have to ski by feeling your way down the hill. Take turns leading and following—or, ski in your partner's dust all day and you will be amazed at the improvement in your sensitivity to the snow and terrain.

A variation of this drill is to put tape across the bottom half of your goggle lenses. You will be able to see the distance but not immediately in front of you. This will also improve your feel and sensitivity.

Drill 5: SKIING THE CRUD

Crud is a term for old powder, wind-blown snow, or cut-up powder. Many skiers avoid the crud. Skiing in these conditions requires excellent balance and at the same time improves balance. When starting out, work into it slowly. Stay forward. Feel the weight on the balls of your feet and pressure against the fronts of your boots. Keep the skis evenly weighted and pressured. Try to keep your leg muscles relaxed. And smile—it helps!

Dynamic Movement Drills

Skiing is a dynamic movement sport. Many skiers never progress to advanced skiing because they never get out of static positions. Learning to move dynamically through and between turns will assist in putting the versatility and adaptability in your skiing that will lead to the far reaches of high-performance skiing.

Drill 1: FLOW TURNS

Find a run with beginner terrain and groomed snow. Standing at the top of the run, relax as much as possible. Now, push off and begin making easy, relaxed, medium-radius turns. Continue making turns while keeping as relaxed as possible. Concentrate on all movements being relaxed and fluid.

Move to a slope with intermediate, groomed terrain. Ski the run with linked, easy turns, focusing on being relaxed and fluid. Don't worry about how you look, just be relaxed. Progress to more demanding terrain while feeling little muscle tension. Remember the feelings. As you ski in more demanding terrain and situations, recall the relaxed and fluid feelings and try to keep them in your skiing.

Drill 2: LEAPERS

Extension and flexion movements are critical for weight transfer, edge control, pressure control, and dynamic balancing. This drill will help you develop more up-and-down movements in your skiing. Use a smooth, intermediate slope and ski at a moderate speed. Cross the hill in a traverse and then leap upward, lifting the skis off the snow. While the skis are in the air, turn the body and skis. Land, and finish the turn into a new traverse. Repeat to the other side. Practice leaping higher with increasing direction change while the skis are in the air. This drill exaggerates your motion and improves tight and static skiing (see figure 9.13).

Try this drill in moguls. Spring off the top of a mogul, turn the skis in the air, and land gently in the trough below the mogul. For variety, leap off the top of one mogul and land on the backside of another.

Figure 9.13 Leapers.

This will help create the dynamic extension and flexion movements you need for high-performance mogul skiing.

Drill 3: PERPENDICULAR BODY

Keeping your body perpendicular to your skis and the snow at all times will help you maintain a balanced stance despite changing terrain. Find a trail that has rolls, short pitches, and drop-offs. Ski the trail without stopping, being sure that every time the terrain changes, you anticipate the change by moving your body forward. This will keep you perpendicular at all times (see figure 9.14).

Try the same drill in moguls. As soon as you ski over the mogul, move forward so your body is perpendicular to the skis on the down side of the mogul. This will immediately improve your mogul skiing.

Figure 9.14 Perpendicular body.

Drill 4: SKIING ON ONE SKI

Start on a groomed beginner slope. Ski a series of linked, short-radius turns using only the left ski, while keeping the right ski up in the air. To do this, you will need to experiment with balance, weight transfer, and pressure control. Switch and ski only on the right ski (see figure 9.15). Move to an intermediate slope and continue with the one-ski drill. Work on making turns without stopping and skiing challenging terrain. Most good ski racers have spent hours doing this drill in order to hone their balance, and their edging and pressure skills.

The drills described above, and others you may learn in ski school, a skiing workshop, or ski racing camp, will help you correct technical problems, refine skills, and enhance skiing performance. All good

Figure 9.15 Skiing on one ski.

skiers have a small set of skill drills they do to warm up, tune up, or just take the rust off their skiing. Develop your own set of drills that fits your strengths, weaknesses, and skiing challenges. Work on them often and you will continue your progress in your high-performance skiing.

SKI SCHOOL

Every ski resort in the United States (and most resorts worldwide) offers a school with instructors trained to teach skiing at a variety of levels. If the ski school is affiliated with the Professional Ski Instructors of America (PSIA), you can be assured that its instructors teach up-to-date methods for skier development. Instruction can benefit your high-performance skiing.

Why Should You Take a Ski School Class?

Let's clear up a common misconception: ski school classes are not just for beginners; they exist for all levels of skiers. In fact, your presence in an upper-level ski school class is more a statement of your skiing ability and willingness to learn than your inability and timidity. Many skiers in beginning and lower-level classes lack skills, are scared of some aspects of the sport, and are insecure on skis; however, there is a great deal to be gained by taking a ski school class, particularly if you are an upper-level skier.

Ski school instructors continually take classes (clinics) from other more skilled and trained instructors (clinicians); World Cup and Olympic racers have coaches; coaches have clinics. Skiing is a sport of constant learning. The best skiers in the world learned the basics before becoming high-performance skiers, and they continually work on basics and their individual skiing skills. Advanced ski school lessons and workshops are excellent sources of learning from the experts.

What to Expect of a Ski School Class or Workshop

A ski school class should offer an expert arrangement of three keys to rev up your skiing: recognition, exposure, and guidance.

• Recognition: you learn about how you ski: correctly or incorrectly; efficiently or inefficiently.

- Exposure: you are exposed to the fundamentals of skiing through a progression of exercises and drills that help you expand on your foundation of skiing skills. When you are well-grounded in the basics, new movements that you learn in more advanced ski lessons can lead to dramatic improvements in your skiing.

- Guidance: explore a variety of adaptations in your skiing through the instructor, your exposure to the movements you are asked to perform, and your interaction with others in the class. By accepting guidance and enjoying learning, you can discover the style of skiing that suits you—an open-ended, no-style perspective to your skiing is advantageous because it allows you to evolve and change.

Selecting the Correct Class

Be honest in assessing your skill level and talk candidly with ski school personnel to determine which class is right for you. Once a class has begun, your instructor or a ski school supervisor may reassess your skiing and suggest you be placed in another class for a more appropriate learning experience. If it's a lower level class, you may find yourself battling with your ego for self-respect; it is best to defer to your best interests and admit that your skiing lacks some of the basics, which the trained eye of the instructor noticed when he or she watched you ski. Understand that these deficiencies may exist even though we may not recognize or feel them in our skiing.

If you have trouble with one level of skills (e.g., making parallel turns on smooth terrain), don't try to get into a higher level class (e.g., parallel turns in all terrain) for the challenge of it, even if your friend or spouse does—you'll have the tendency to rely on slope survival tactics instead of skiing skills. The search for a challenge is the wrong reason to take a ski school class.

Many ski schools offer workshops for advanced skiers, usually led by the more experienced and trained instructors. There may be workshops for moguls, powder skiing, recreational racing, all-mountain discovery, and women. You will be grouped with other skiers of similar ability and skill levels. Workshops may be as short as a half day and as long as a week, and may be just what you need to reach your goals in high-performance skiing.

Taking a Private Lesson

Private lessons can satisfy an individual's or family's specific ski performance needs, and are suited to the shy skier who is uncomfortable in groups. Private lessons may not be appropriate for learning the fundamentals; group lessons are more economical and provide psychological support while on the slopes. You may request a particular instructor, usually in hourly increments. The courteous and smart thing to do is book the instructor a day or two in advance to make sure his or her schedule is clear. How do you choose an instructor for a private lesson? You are your most important resource. If you had a group lesson with an instructor whom you perceive to have appealing teaching qualities, then a private lesson from this instructor might prove to be a valuable experience. Tips from friends and other instructors can help you select an instructor for a private lesson, or you can seek out instructors that you have read about in a magazine or book, seen on television, or heard about via other skiers' chatter in the lodge or chalet. You may also present your particular skill problem to a ski school supervisor, who will help select an instructor who is right for you.

Getting the Most Out of a Ski School Class

When you take ski school lessons you will want to know that you are getting the best value for your money. Much of what you get out of a lesson depends on your expectations and what you put into the lesson.

Go into the class (or clinic or race camp) with the attitude that you are supplementing your skiing by giving yourself opportunities to refine your skills through recognition, exposure, and guidance. If it's early in the season, you may want to use the class to get reacquainted with your skis and the basic skills. If you are adventurous, consider taking classes to study the condition of the day. For example, if there is a day with new-fallen snow, most of the upper-level classes will concern powder or at least deal with powder skills. If you are deficient in powder skills, this would be a perfect day to take a lesson.

Make ski school classes work for you. Use them to complement your efforts to solve problems in your skiing; be open to other problems that are revealed to you by an astute instructor or merciless video. Videos can be ruthless intrusions into our fantasy about how we see ourselves skiing. If you can overcome the tendency to remember how awful you look, and concentrate instead on the areas of skill improvement, videos can be an excellent tool for achieving greater performance in your skiing. If you weaken for a moment, however, videos can devastate even the sturdiest of egos and give you the wrong mental images with which to go skiing.

Keep these eight points in mind during class.

1. Be an open vessel; that is, assume no skill level, no bias, and no prejudice, and listen to everything the instructor and other students say.

2. Don't go into the class assuming that you are the best or worst skier in the class; your ego will interfere with learning.

3. Don't make assumptions; ask questions and seek clarification of drills and exercises.

4. Don't assume that everything the instructor says is scripture.

5. Have a physical attitude about the class; that is, try the exercises and drills demonstrated by the instructor, performing them as perfectly as you can. As a rule, most skiing skills are learned by exaggerated movements that, when done collectively, produce a skill. Exercises and drills are often designed to provide repetitions of exaggerated movements until the correct movements become second nature and the skill is firmly established in your skiing.

6. Expect some exercises and drills to be difficult and to feel awkward at first, making you look like a less-than-advanced skier. Other drills will boost your and others' opinions of your skiing. Your success in performing the drills will come with continued effort, not avoidance.

A common complaint of disgruntled ski school students is that they feel they don't learn enough from classes. A frequent complaint from ski school instructors is that too few students make a serious effort to do the exercises and drills. Most of the exercises and drills given to you in ski school have undergone a great deal of experimentation on the slopes. They have been designed to follow a certain progression, taking you from familiar to unfamiliar movements that accompany your acquisition of a new skill. Avoiding drills because they seem difficult or embarrassing is a waste of your ski school dollar as well as precious skiing time.

7. Know the mind-set that must accompany the physical attitude. For the effect and benefit of the exercises, avoid the tendency to make your exercises or drills exhibitions of your wonderful skiing skills for instructor and students alike. Such ego involvement obfuscates the value of the exercises.

8. Think of yourself as a perfect learner, a perfect student of skiing. Listen attentively and try to understand what is being said. Ask

questions when you don't understand what has been said or when you are confused about a kinesthetic feeling that you notice in relation to an exercise or drill. Pay attention to why something is happening to your skis, what is going on in your body, when this is happening, and what happens when you repeat the action. Be aware of the feeling of performing a task awkwardly and then more fluidly. Glean something from the class (a drill, exercise, perspective) to use for practice in your everyday skiing.

Assume that you learned some drills about separating your upper and lower body while skiing. Which drill should you take from the class? All of them? The easiest? The most difficult? You can't realistically take all of the drills, so take the one(s) that will help you the most: the most difficult. The difficulty of a drill often reveals a significant problem with particular aspects of your skiing.

When you take a difficult drill from class, perform it on a gentle slope until you can do it well. Vary and upgrade the terrain in which you practice your drills as long as you can perform them as intended. Drills that were easy in class can be done on increasingly difficult terrain. Taking drills from classes and practicing them on your own is the way to get the most out of your ski school class and ensure improvement in your skiing.

KEYS TO HIGH PERFORMANCE

1. The key to improving is recognizing problems and skill errors and challenging yourself to correct them.
2. Often by correcting a balance problem you will automatically correct an error or be able to perform a skill correctly.
3. Perfect practice makes perfect. When performing drills, exercises, or high-performance skiing, work toward perfection to benefit the most.
4. Continually practice basic drills to improve your skills.
5. Work on pole-plants for timing, balance, and re-centering. Properly executed pole-plants will enhance your skiing in any situation.
6. Angulation and proper edge angles will help you carve turns and ski efficiently.
7. Steering at the beginning of the turn will facilitate turn initiation and help maintain balance.

8. Adding versatility to your high-performance skiing will allow you to enjoy skiing in most situations.

9. Ski school classes, workshops, and private lessons can enhance the skiing skills of even advanced high-performance skiers.

10. Target ski school classes, workshops, or specialty clinics to your own interests and to specific areas in which you want to improve.

INDEX

ABOUT THE AUTHORS

John Yacenda wrote the first edition of *High-Performance Skiing* as well as the successful *Alpine Skiing: Steps to Success*. Both of these books marked a clear departure from conventional skiing instruction by stressing the importance of the "inside ski" in ski technique, a concept now fully accepted in the sport. He also writes two syndicated columns, "Skiing" and "Ski Tips."

Yacenda has been a professional and private ski instructor, and has taught a preseason conditioning program for racers and other skiers for more than 10 years.

Yacenda is the CEO and director of the Great Basin Primary Care Association in Carson City, Nevada. He lives in Reno with his wife, Benita. In his leisure time he enjoys cross-training, playing guitar and writing music, and traveling and exploring.

Tim Ross has been professionally involved in skiing and ski racing for more than 25 years. As the director of coaches' education for U.S. Skiing since 1988, Ross has worked with the best ski coaches and teaching professionals in the country. He has coached at World Cup races, World Junior Championships, and World Alpine Championships. He is also editor of *The American Ski Coach*, the official journal of the U.S. Ski Coaches Association.

Ross Lives in Park City, Utah, with his wife, Karin. In his leisure time he enjoys climbing, mountaineering, and mountain biking.

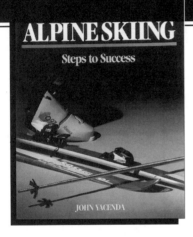

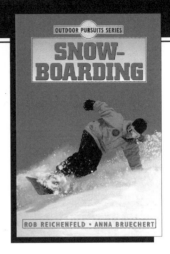